*The Quotable*
## NATHAN BEDFORD FORREST

BOOKS BY LOCHLAINN SEABROOK

A Rebel Born: A Defense of Nathan Bedford Forrest - Confederate General, American Legend (winner of the 2011 Jefferson Davis Historical Gold Medal)
Nathan Bedford Forrest: Southern Hero, American Patriot - Honoring a Confederate Icon and the Old South
The Quotable Nathan Bedford Forrest: Selections From the Writings and Speeches of the Confederacy's Most Brilliant Cavalryman
Give 'Em Hell Boys! The Complete Military Correspondence of Nathan Bedford Forrest
Everything You Were Taught About the Civil War is Wrong, Ask a Southerner! - Correcting the Errors of Yankee "History"
The Quotable Jefferson Davis: Selections From the Writings and Speeches of the Confederacy's First President
The Quotable Robert E. Lee: Selections From the Writings and Speeches of the South's Most Beloved Civil War General
The Old Rebel: Robert E. Lee As He Was Seen By His Contemporaries
Abraham Lincoln: The Southern View - Demythologizing America's Sixteenth President
Lincolnology: The Real Abraham Lincoln Revealed in His Own Words - A Study of Lincoln's Suppressed, Misinterpreted, and Forgotten Speeches and Writings
The Unquotable Abraham Lincoln: The President's Quotes They Don't Want You To Know!
Encyclopedia of the Battle of Franklin - A Comprehensive Guide to the Conflict that Changed the Civil War
Carnton Plantation Ghost Stories: True Tales of the Unexplained from Tennessee's Most Haunted Civil War House!
The McGavocks of Carnton Plantation: A Southern History - Celebrating One of Dixie's Most Noble Confederate Families and Their Tennessee Home
The Caudills: An Etymological, Ethnological, and Genealogical Study - Exploring the Name and National Origins of a European-American Family
The Blakeneys: An Etymological, Ethnological, and Genealogical Study - Uncovering the Mysterious Origins of the Blakeney Family and Name
Britannia Rules: Goddess-Worship in Ancient Anglo-Celtic Society - An Academic Look at the United Kingdom's Matricentric Spiritual Past
UFOs and Aliens: The Complete Guidebook
Christmas Before Christianity: How the Birthday of the "Sun" Became the Birthday of the "Son"
The Book of Kelle: An Introduction to Goddess-Worship and the Great Celtic Mother-Goddess Kelle, Original Blessed Lady of Ireland
The Goddess Dictionary of Words and Phrases: Introducing a New Core Vocabulary for the Women's Spirituality Movement
Aphrodite's Trade: The Hidden History of Prostitution Unveiled

*Thought Provoking Books For Smart People*
**www.SeaRavenPress.com**

*The Quotable*

# NATHAN BEDFORD FORREST

*Selections From the Writings and Speeches of the Confederacy's Most Brilliant Cavalryman*

Collected and Edited, with an Introduction and Notes, by

# LOCHLAINN SEABROOK

**WINNER OF THE JEFFERSON DAVIS HISTORICAL GOLD MEDAL**

Sea Raven Press, Franklin, Tennessee, USA

# THE QUOTABLE NATHAN BEDFORD FORREST

Published by
Sea Raven Press, P.O. Box 1054, Franklin, Tennessee 37065-1054 USA
www.searavenpress.com • searavenpress@nii.net

Copyright © 2012 Lochlainn Seabrook
in accordance with U.S. and international copyright laws and regulations, as stated and protected under the Berne Union for the Protection of Literary and Artistic Property (Berne Convention), and the Universal Copyright Convention (the UCC). All rights reserved under the Pan-American and International Copyright Conventions.

First Sea Raven Press Civil War Sesquicentennial Edition: January 2012
ISBN: 978-0-9838185-5-7
Library of Congress Catalog Number: 2011944856

This work is the copyrighted intellectual property of Lochlainn Seabrook and has been registered with the Copyright Office at the Library of Congress in Washington, D.C., USA. No part of this work (including text, covers, drawings, photos, illustrations, maps, images, diagrams, etc.), in whole or in part, may be used, reproduced, stored in a retrieval system, or transmitted, in any form or by any means now known or hereafter invented, without written permission from the publisher. The sale, duplication, hire, lending, copying, digitalization, or reproduction of this material, in any manner or form whatsoever, is also prohibited, and is a violation of federal, civil, and digital copyright law, which provides severe civil and criminal penalties for any violations.

The Quotable Nathan Bedford Forrest: Selections From the Writings and Speeches of the Confederacy's Most Brilliant Cavalryman / collected and edited, with an introduction and notes, by Lochlainn Seabrook. Includes bibliographical references.

*Front and back cover design, book design and layout, by Lochlainn Seabrook*
*Typography: Sea Raven Press Book Design*
*Front cover image "Nathan Bedford Forrest" © Chris Rommel*
*Sketch of the author on "Meet the Author" page © Tracy Latham*
*All images are from 19th-Century public domain sources, unless otherwise indicated*
*(Portions of this book have been adapted from the author's other works.)*

The views on the American "Civil War" documented in this book *are* those of the publisher.

The paper used in this book is acid-free and lignin-free. It has been certified by the Sustainable Forestry Initiative and the Forest Stewardship Council and meets all ANSI standards for archival quality paper.

PRINTED & MANUFACTURED IN OCCUPIED TENNESSEE, FORMER CONFEDERATE STATES OF AMERICA

# *Dedication*

To my cousin, the Wizard of the Saddle

# Epigraph

"If Forrest had had the advantages of a thorough military education and training, he would have been the great central figure of the Civil War."

General Joseph E. Johnston, C.S.A.

# CONTENTS

*Notes to the Reader* - 8
*Introduction, by Lochlainn Seabrook* - 9

### SECTION ONE: ANTEBELLUM PERIOD
1 CHILDHOOD & ADULTHOOD: 1807-1845 - 15
2 MARRIAGE & FATHERHOOD: 1845-1877 - 17

### SECTION TWO: BELLUM PERIOD, LINCOLN'S WAR
3 CONFEDERATE ARMY LIFE: 1861-1865 - 23
4 MILITARY REPORTS & DISPATCHES: 1861-1865 - 39

### SECTION THREE: POSTBELLUM PERIOD
5 YANKEE NEWSPAPER INTERVIEW: 1868 - 97
6 JOINT SELECT COMMITTEE INTERROGATION: 1871 - 104
7 LAST YEARS : 1866-1877 - 113

*Notes* - 119
*Bibliography* - 123
*Meet the Author* - 125
*Meet the Cover Artist* - 128

# NOTES TO THE READER

🖐 In an effort to retain the true character and meaning of General Forrest's words, they have been printed here exactly as they appear in the original manuscripts, including typographical and grammatical peculiarities inherent to both Forrest and to 19$^{th}$-Century American writing and speaking (in some cases I have broken up long paragraphs). Quotes are marked with a traditional Victorian "hand" pointer. My chapter introductions are in normal font, my explanatory comments appear in italics above the writers' quotes, and my clarifications are in brackets within their quotes.

🖐 In any study of the "Civil War" it is vitally important to keep in mind that the two major political parties were then the opposite of what they are today. The Democrats of the mid 19$^{th}$ Century were conservatives, akin to the Republican Party of today, while the Republicans of the mid 19$^{th}$ Century were liberals, akin to the Democratic Party of today. Thus the Confederacy's Democratic president, Jefferson Davis, was a conservative (with libertarian leanings); the Union's Republican president, Abraham Lincoln, was a liberal (with socialistic leanings).

🖐 For those interested in the truth about the War for Southern Independence, see my books:

*A Rebel Born: A Defense of Nathan Bedford Forrest - Confederate General, American Legend*
*Nathan Bedford Forrest: Southern Hero, American Patriot - Honoring a Confederate Icon and the Old South*
*Give 'Em Hell Boys! The Complete Military Correspondence of Nathan Bedford Forrest*
*Everything You Were Taught About the Civil War is Wrong, Ask a Southerner! - Correcting the Errors of Yankee "History"*
*The Quotable Robert E. Lee: Selections From the Writings and Speeches of the South's Most Beloved Civil War General*
*The Old Rebel: Robert E. Lee As He Was Seen By His Contemporaries*
*The Quotable Jefferson Davis: Selections From the Writings & Speeches of the Confederacy's First President*
*Abraham Lincoln: The Southern View - Demythologizing America's Sixteenth President*
*Lincolnology: The Real Abraham Lincoln Revealed in His Own Words - A Study of Lincoln's Suppressed, Misinterpreted, and Forgotten Speeches and Writings*
*The Unquotable Abraham Lincoln: The President's Quotes They Don't Want You to Know!*
*The McGavocks of Carnton Plantation: A Southern History - Celebrating One of Dixie's Most Noble Confederate Families and Their Tennessee Home*
*Carnton Plantation Ghost Stories: True Tales of the Unexplained from Tennessee's Most Haunted Civil War House!*

# INTRODUCTION

I have covered most of the salient points of Forrest's life in my other three works: the award-winning *A Rebel Born: A Defense of Nathan Bedford Forrest*, *Nathan Bedford Forrest: Southern Hero, American Patriot*, and *Give 'Em Hell Boys! The Complete Military Correspondence of Nathan Bedford Forrest*. However, there is always more to say about the South's favorite Confederate cavalryman!

For one thing, I felt that my cousin deserved a work that consolidated his more noteworthy statements. This book is the result.

"The Wizard of the Saddle," as we love to call him here in the South, was not a writer, he wrote few personal letters (and scarcely any of these remain), and he never authored a book. Though he had a genius IQ, he was not college-educated, he was not a professional speaker, and he never gave a lecture. Nonetheless, he did make a number of memorable statements throughout his life and he filed countless military reports during Lincoln's War. Fortunately for us, many of his friends, business associates, and biographers thought to preserve some of these for posterity. It is around this surviving material that this book was created.

It is my hope that *The Quotable Nathan Bedford Forrest*, like my other three books on the General, will introduce him to new readers, help destroy the numerous absurd and slanderous Northern myths surrounding him, and bring him out of the shadows and into the mainstream of American history where he justly belongs.

As Forrest's own words show, he was not an "illiterate inbred hillbilly," a "monstrous racist," or a "cruel and violent slave owner," as the North and New South disingenuously continue to preach. Quite the opposite.

He was, as Confederate General Richard Taylor said of him, a "tenderhearted, kindly man,"[1] a true Southern gentleman, a fair and compassionate Rebel officer, a successful businessman, and a faithful husband who loved children, protected women, and gave charitably to war veterans, orphans, and widows. A traditional conservative Southerner and a staunch supporter of states' rights who freed his slaves years before "King Abraham's" fraudulent Emancipation Proclamation was issued, unlike the North, he stood firmly behind our country's most sacred document, the Constitution—before, during, and after Lincoln's War.

For these reasons, and a thousand more, Nathan Bedford Forrest has earned my lifelong love, respect, and admiration, and I am proud to be his kin. He deserves to have many more *honest* and *objective* books written about him.

Lochlainn Seabrook
Franklin, Williamson County, Tennessee, USA
January 2012, Civil War Sesquicentennial

One of America's many monuments to General Nathan Bedford Forrest. This one, his beautiful and famous equestrian statue at Forrest Park, Memphis, Tennessee, marks the General's grave site. Traditional Southerners and lovers of the Constitution rightly consider the spot a holy shrine.

# The Quotable
# NATHAN BEDFORD FORREST

# SECTION ONE

# ANTEBELLUM PERIOD

# CHILDHOOD AND ADULTHOOD
## 1807-1845

Nathan Bedford Forrest was born on July 13, 1821, near what is today the beautiful town of Chapel Hill, Bedford (now Marshall) County, Tennessee. His parents were William Forrest and Mariam Beck. His childhood realm was typical of a poor Victorian family of that time and place: the great wilds of Middle Tennessee, then located on America's most western frontier. Thomas Jefferson was still alive, the United States was only forty-five years old, and President James Monroe was in the White House. There are few surviving Forrest quotes from this period.

*Forrest as a boy, after his mother and aunt almost died due to a vicious attack by a mountain lion:*
☞ "Mother, I am going to kill that beast if it stays on the earth."[2]

*On March 10, 1845, at Hernando, Mississippi, a group of four thugs shot and killed Forrest's unarmed Uncle Jonathan. An enraged twenty-four year old Forrest was at the scene and quickly dispatched two of the criminals, while a third escaped. He found the fourth one hiding in a nearby residence, and, dragging him into the street, looked him squarely in the eyes and said:*
☞ "You deserve death at my hands, but I am too brave a man to murder one so completely in my power; I give you your life."[3]

Nathan Bedford Forrest as a young man.

# MARRIAGE & FATHERHOOD
## 1845-1877

William Montgomery Forrest, General Forrest's only son. "Willie," as he was known, named one of his sons Nathan Bedford Forrest II.

Forrest married Mary Ann Montgomery, daughter of William Montgomery and Elizabeth McCroskey Cowan, on September 25, 1845, at Hernando, DeSoto County, Mississippi.

The couple had two children: William Montgomery Forrest (born in 1846) and Francis Ann "Fanny" Forrest (born in 1849). William married (Jane Taylor Cook) and had four children, was a captain in the Confederate army, and lived until 1908. Francis, however, passed away in 1854 at the age of five from flux (dysentery).

The General and Mary Ann remained married for life. She outlived her husband by sixteen years, he passing away in 1877, she in 1893.

*In the Spring of 1845, at Hernando, Mississippi, Forrest unknowingly met his future wife and the mother of his two children, Mary Ann Montgomery. She and her mother, Elizabeth Cowan, were sitting forlornly in a carriage that had become stuck fast in the mud. Nearby, Forrest noticed two men on their horses, watching, but offering no assistance. After carrying the two women to dry land and muscling the carriage free, he turned to the two men and yelled angrily:*

☞ "Why didn't y'all help these ladies? I suggest that you remove yerselves from this vicinity at once, or I'll give you a thrashin' you won't soon fergit!"⁴

*Not long after this episode Forrest began to court Mary Ann, and soon proposed to her. She accepted, but the proposition first had to be cleared with Ann's uncle and legal guardian,⁵ the noted and influential clergyman of the Cumberland Presbyterian Church, Reverend Samuel Montgomery Cowan. Naturally, he was strongly against any marriage between his highly cultivated niece and the rough-and-tumble frontiersman, saying: "Why Bedford, I couldn't consent, you cuss and gamble and Mary Ann is a Christian girl." To this Forrest replied:*

☞ "That's very true sir. And that is exactly why I want to marry her."⁶

*Forrest was very much against drinking, no doubt for the following reason:*

☞ "I was never drunk but once in my life. I had observed the antics of a drunken man, and a strange fancy to try a spell of it took possession of me. I got the liquor and drank it one afternoon. What happened as a consequence I do not know, but when I got over the spree I found myself with a burning case of typhoid fever. I promised 'Old Master' that if he would let me up from that bed I would never get drunk again. And I never broke that pledge."⁷

Jeffrey E. Forrest, Forrest's youngest brother. A brigadier general in the Confederate army, Jeffrey was killed at the Battle of Okolona on February 22, 1864.

*The following is an excerpt from a letter General Forrest wrote to his son, Lieutenant William M. Forrest, during the War:*

☞ ". . . What I must desire of you my son is never to gamble or swear. These are baneful vices and I trust you will never practice either. As I grow older I see the folly of these two vices and beg you will never in engage in them. Your life has heretofore been elevated and characterized by a high-toned morality, and I trust your name will never be stained by the practice of those vices which blighted the prospects of some of the most promising youth of our country. Be honest, be truthful, in all your dealings with the world. Be cautious in the selection of your friends. Shun the society of the low and vulgar. Strive to elevate your character and to take a high and honorable position in society. You are my only child, the pride and hope of my life. You have a fine intellect, talent of the highest order. I have watched your entrance upon the threshold of manhood and life with all the admiration of a proud father, and I trust your future career will be an honor to yourself and a solace to my declining years. If we meet no more on earth I hope you will keep this letter prominently before you and remember it is coming from, Your Affectionate Father."[8]

In the early 1840s General Forrest lived in this home in Hernando, Mississippi. Within a few years his hard work and shrewd business acumen would allow him to leave behind the difficult life of a frontiersman, becoming one of the wealthiest men in the United States. By the time of Lincoln's War in 1861, he was worth an estimated $50 million in today's currency.

General Forrest as he looked during his Confederate officership period. The author of the original caption of this illustration noted that Forrest "was one of the most striking characters developed by the War."

# SECTION TWO

# BELLUM PERIOD
# LINCOLN'S WAR

# CONFEDERATE ARMY LIFE

## 1861-1865

This cavalryman from October 1862 is demonstrating the military command "stand to horse," one that was very familiar to General Forrest's troops.

Though prior to the war Forrest had actually been a "strong Union man" who was against Southern secession, liberal Lincoln's unlawful attack on the conservative South and states' right was too much.[9] A dyed-in-the-wool Southerner, a fervent states' rights advocate, a free-trader, and a Constitutional conservative,[10] Forrest was not going to stand by while Lincoln perverted the Constitution and transformed the government of the Founding Fathers from a confederate republic into a federate empire—one of Lincoln's primary goals.

Thus Forrest wasted no time enlisting in the army in June 1861, at first serving as a private in Captain Josiah S. White's Tennessee Mounted Rifles Company. White's Company constituted Company D in the Sixth Tennessee Battalion (organized on September 7, 1861), later becoming part of the well-known Seventh Tennessee Regiment of Cavalry.[11]

Seeing the appalling lack of supplies, like many other wealthy Confederates, Forrest outfitted, equipped, clothed, armed, and fed his soldiers wherever and whenever he could, all without any aid from the Confederate government.[12] In one case, for instance, he advanced his quartermaster and commissary $20,000 from his own "private funds" for Colt's navy pistols, saddles, and other supplies, the equivalent of about $430,000 today.[13]

His naturally keen grasp of military tactics, along with his elevated socioeconomic status (there were not many multimillionaire privates in the Confederate Army!) and sterling recommendations from the citizens of Memphis, impressed both Governor Isham Greene Harris, Tennessee's only Confederate governor, and Bishop-General Leonidas Polk.

Soon, despite his lack of military training, Forrest won a promotion to colonel. His star continued to rise quickly and by October he was commanding his own regiment, "Forrest's Tennessee Cavalry Battalion."

He was also an excellent recruiter. Hundreds of Tennesseans, young and old, eagerly joined the Confederate army under Forrest's rousing promise that there would be "ample opportunity to kill Yankees." A natural born leader and sagacious tactician, before the War was over Forrest would become the only man on either side to go from private to lieutenant general.

*Since Lincoln wanted war, Dixie's sons had no choice but to fight. Many Southerners felt just as Forrest did, as he would later say in an 1868 interview:*
☞ "I went into the war because my vote had been unable to preserve the peace."[14]

*One of General Forrest's many battle cries:*
☞ "Forward, men, and mix with 'em!"[15]

*In mid February 1862, after realizing that the Confederacy would probably unnecessarily lose Fort Donelson to the Yanks, Forrest told his "fightin' preacher," Major David C. Kelley:*
☞ "Parson, for God's sake, pray! Nothin' but God Almighty can save that fort!"[16]

*Forrest's words to his troops after telling his commanders at Fort Donelson that he*

Forrest's chief of artillery, Captain John W. Morton, in a charge against the enemy.

would not surrender:
☞ "We're going out even if we die in the attempt!"[17]

When told by a Yank that Union General James Harrison Wilson was a West Point graduate and an excellent tactician, Forrest replied:
☞ "Wal, I never rubbed my back up agin a college, an' I don't profess to know much about tactics, but I'd give more for fifteen minutes of the 'bulge' on you than for three days of tactics."[18]

*When asked if it was possible to fight and win a battle without loss of life, Forrest replied:*
☞ "War means fightin', and fightin' means killin'."[19]

*Surveying the smouldering ruins of a Yankee war depot after the Battle of Johnsonville, November 4-5, 1864, Forrest told his Chief of Artillery John W. Morton:*
☞ "There is no doubt we could soon wipe old Sherman off the face of the earth, John, if they'd give me enough men and you enough guns."[20]

*The following is an example of one of Forrest's orders to his men:*
☞ "Whenever you meet the enemy, show fight, no matter how few there are of you or how many of them, show fight. If you run away they will pursue and probably catch you. If you show fight, they will think there are more of you, and will not push you half so hard."[21]

*Forrest was once asked about his formula for winning battles:*
☞ "I do not know, unless it was because I generally got there first with the most men."[22]

*Two of Forrest's many famous maxims, often repeated to his men on the battlefield:*
☞ "Shoot at anythin' blue, and keep up the skeer!"[23]

*After capturing a Yankee preacher and holding him overnight, Forrest decided to release him back to the Union lines the next day. The General left the clergyman with these parting words:*
☞ "Parson, I would keep you here to preach for me if you were not needed so much more by the sinners on the other side."[24]

*Forrest to his Chief-of-Staff Major Charles W. Anderson at the Battle of Brice's Cross Roads:*
☞ "Tell [Confederate General Tyree H.] Bell to move up fast and fetch all he's got."[25]

*One of Forrest's numerous battle rules, often relayed to his men:*
☞ "Never stand and take a charge from the enemy. Charge them

too!"[26]

*Forrest to Major Charles W. Anderson just prior to the Battle of Dover (also known as the Battle of Fort Donelson II), in February 1863:*

Major Gilbert Vincent Rambaut, Forrest's chief commissary.

☞ "I have a special request to make of you in regard to the proposed attack on Fort Donelson. I have protested against this move, but my protest has been disregarded, and I intend to do my whole duty, and I want my men to do the same. I have spoken to none but you on this subject, and I do not wish that any one should know of the objections I have made. I have this request to make: If I am killed in this fight, you will see that justice is done me by officially stating that I protested against the attack, and that I am not willing to be held responsible for any disaster that may result."[27]

*In the Spring of 1863 Forrest and his cavalry rode and fought for five days and nights, traversing some 150 miles of mountainous terrain nearly non-stop, capturing an entire Yankee command of 1,600 men, nearly four times the size of his own. The Union commander, General Able D. Streight, was not amused with Forrest's "braggin' and bluffin'" mode of fighting. Forrest describes the scene:*
☞ "When Streight saw they [my troops] were barely four hundred, he did rear! Demanded to have his arms back and that we should fight it out. I just laughed at him and patted him on the shoulder, and said, 'Ah, Colonel, all is fair in love and war, you know.'"[28]

*Once, when one of Forrest's officers made the mistake of asking him for a furlough twice, he got this reply from the General scrawled on the back of the application:*
☞ "I told you twixt goddamn it, know!"[29]

Forrest to Confederate General James R. Chalmers in April 1862, prior to the disastrous Battle of Shiloh:
☞ "If this army does not move and attack them between this and daylight, and before other reinforcements arrive, it will be whipped like hell before ten o'clock to-morrow."[30]

Forrest only got drunk once in his life, a miserable experience that he came to regret. Thus, whenever the teetotaler was invited to imbibe, he always gave the same answer:
☞ "My staff does all my drinking for me."[31]

On May 2, 1863, at Black Creek, on the road between Blountsville and Gadsden, Alabama, Forrest found that Union General Able D. Streight had crossed the only bridge in the area and burned it behind him. While Forrest was pondering his next move he came upon a young lass named Emma Sansom, who told him of a "lost ford" downstream. The Yanks had taken all of her family's horses, but she would be happy to lead him to it. With no time to lose and bullets flying around them, Forrest pulled the youngster up onto his saddle, yelling out to her mother:
☞ "She is going to show me a ford where I can get my men over in time to catch those Yankees before they get to Rome. Don't be uneasy; I will bring her back safe!"[32]

Before riding off to continue his pursuit of Streight, Forrest left this note behind for Emma:
☞ "Hed Quaters in Sadle, May 2, 1863: My highest regardes to Miss Ema Sansom for hir gallant conduct while my posse was skirmishing with the Federals a cross Black Creek near Gadsden Allabama. N. B. Forrest, Brig. Genl. Comding N. Ala."[33]

Once, during a skirmish in Mississippi, Forrest caught a cowardly soldier fleeing from the front lines. After giving the poor boy a solid thrashing with a tree branch, he yelled:
☞ "Now—damn you, go back to the front and fight: you might as well be killed there as here, for if you ever run away again you will not get off so easy."[34]

On June 13, 1863, one of Forrest's soldiers, Lieutenant Andrew Wills Gould,

*tracked down his commander in Columbia, Tennessee, and tried to kill him with a small weapon. The reason? The young impetuous Gould felt his character had been impugned by Forrest during an earlier encounter.*[35] *After Gould shot Forrest, the two scuffled. Gould lost control of his gun, enabling Forrest to inflict a mortal wound with a small knife. As Gould fled, Forrest took off in pursuit yelling:*
☞ "Damn it, no one kills me and lives to tell about it!"[36]

*Limping back to his headquarters nearby, a doctor rushed to the scene and suggested that Forrest be immediately taken to the hospital, whereupon Forrest shouted:*
☞ "It's nothin' but a damned little pistol ball! Let it be!"[37]

*On September 28, 1863, General Braxton Bragg angrily relieved Forrest of his command over negative comments he had made about Bragg's conduct at the Battle of Chickamauga. Worse still, Bragg turned the command over to someone Forrest did not respect: General Joseph Wheeler. In a rage, Forrest sent off an angry note to Bragg, charging him with "duplicity" and "lying." After he watched the courier ride off with the missive, Forrest told one of his aides:*
☞ "Bragg never got such a letter as that before from a brigadier."[38]

Colonel James W. Starnes served under Forrest in the Fourth Tennessee Cavalry, Commanding Brigade.

*A few days later, on October 1, 1863, Forrest went directly to General Bragg at his headquarters at Missionary Ridge, Chattanooga, Tennessee. Here a bitter personal confrontation ensued, at which Forrest said the following to his superior:*
☞ "I am not here to pass civilities or compliments with you, but on other business. You commenced your cowardly and contemptible persecution of me soon after the battle of Shiloh, and you have kept it up ever since. You did it because I reported to Richmond facts, while you reported damn lies. You robbed

me of my command in Kentucky and gave it to one of your favorites—men that I armed and equipped from the enemies of our country. In a spirit of revenge and spite, because I would not fawn upon you as others did, you drove me into West Tennessee in the winter of 1862, with a second brigade I had organized, with improper arms and without sufficient ammunition, although I had made repeated applications for the same. You did it to ruin me and my career. When, in spite of all this, I returned with my command, well equipped by captures, you began again your work of spite and persecution, and have kept it up; and now this second brigade, organized and equipped without thanks to you or the government, a brigade which has won a reputation for successful fighting second to none in the army, taking advantage of your position as the commanding general in order to further humiliate me, you have taken these brave men from me. I have stood your meanness as long as I intend to. You have played the part of a damn scoundrel, and are a coward; and if you were any part of a man, I would slap your jaws and force you to resent it. You may as well not issue any more orders to me, for I will not obey them, and I will hold you personally responsible for any further indignities you endeavor to inflict upon me. You have threatened to arrest me for not obeying your orders promptly. I dare you to do it, and I say to you that if you ever again try to interfere with me or cross my path it will be at the peril of your life.'[39]

*After Forrest's argument with Bragg, Forrest's Chief Surgeon, Dr. James B. Cowan, said to him, "Well, you are in for it now!", to which the General replied:*
☞ "He'll never say a word about it; he'll be the last man to mention it; and, mark my word, he'll take no action in the matter."[40]

*In January 1863, when Forrest and his men found themselves near Clifton, Tennessee, surrounded on at least two sides by advancing Yanks, one of his subordinates, Colonel Charles Carroll, called out frantically, "What shall we do General?" Above the din of whistling bullets Forrest yelled back:*
☞ "Charge 'em both ways!"[41]

*From an address by Forrest to his troops in early 1865:*
☞ "If your course has been marked by the graves of patriotic heroes who have fallen by your side, it has, at the same time, been more plainly

marked by the blood of the invader. While you sympathize with the friends of the fallen, your sorrows should be appeased by the knowledge that they fell as brave men battling for all that makes life worth living for."[42]

*Often soldiers reported to Forrest for duty freshly released from the hospital or as newly exchanged prisoners of war, always without weapons. Operating on the principle that an unarmed soldier was better than no soldier at all (for this made his effective fighting force look larger), Forrest sent these men right into battle, even if their only weapon was the Rebel Yell (which helped intimidate the enemy, he rightly asserted). To those who hesitated at what they perceived as sheer madness, Forrest had this to say:*

☞ "Just follow along here, we'll have a fight presently, and then you can git plenty of guns and ammunition from the Yankees."[43]

A postwar picture of Tennessean Brigadier General George G. Dibrell, who served under Forrest in the Eighth Tennessee Cavalry.

*Throughout Lincoln's illegitimate and needless four-year conflict, between 300,000 and 1 million African-Americans (according to the definition of a "private soldier" as determined by Yankee General August V. Kautz) fought courageously for the Confederacy[44] alongside their European-American brethren (their exact number will never be known because Yankees, like war criminal General Edward Hatch,[45] specifically targeted Southern courthouses—where records were kept—for burning).[46] This should not be surprising: Dixie was, after all, their homeland as well, and the only one they had ever known. Among the hundreds of thousands of black Confederates were sixty-five slaves serving under Forrest, forty-five of them belonging to the dashing officer himself.[47] Throughout 1864*

*Forrest energetically continued his black impressment and enrollment program, as the following example from his headquarters at Okolona, Mississippi (dated August 5, 1864), reveals. Note that Forrest intended to use these particular blacks, not as slave laborers as Lincoln did when he first reluctantly enlisted African-Americans, but as regular armed soldiers:*

☞ ". . . all that can be done shall be done in North Mississippi to drive the enemy back. At the same time I have not the force to risk a general engagement, and will resort to all other means in my reach to harass, annoy, and force the enemy back. I have ordered the impressment of negroes for the purpose of fortifying positions, blockading roads and fords upon the rivers, and shall strike him in flank and rear, and oppose him in front to the extent of my ability and fight him at all favorable positions along his line of march."[48]

*One of Forrest's numerous tricks was to simply order his German bugler, Jacob Gaus, to blow the call for his men to form a circle:*

☞ "I will often have need of this maneuver as it will be necessary from time to time for me to show more men than I actually have on the field."[49]

*Contrary to popular belief, Lincoln's treatment of blacks during his war was far from what one would expect from the "Great Emancipator." For example, not only did he pay his black soldiers half of what he paid his white soldiers, he also denied African-American military men pensions, bounties, and bonuses, all which were provided to white Union soldiers. Lincoln even ordered that medical attention be given to whites first. Additionally, rather than issuing freedmen "forty acres and a mule" as he had falsely promised,[50] he decided instead to pen them up like livestock in "government corrals," and withhold food, clothing, and medical care from them. On September 26, 1864, at the Brown Farm at Elkton, Tennessee (near Pulaski), Forrest came across one of these squalid U.S. black camps[51] and described it like this:*

☞ "From Elkton I directed my course toward a Government corral at Brown's plantation, toward Pulaski. At this place I found about 2,000 negroes, consisting mostly of old men, women, and children, besides a large amount of commissary stores and medical supplies. General Buford having completed his work at Elk River joined me at this place, where I issued to my entire command several days' rations, distributing among the troops as much sugar and coffee as they needed. The negroes were all ragged and dirty, and many seemed in absolute want. I ordered them to remove their clothing and bed clothes from the miserable hovels in which they lived and then burnt up this den of wretchedness. Near 200 houses were consumed."⁵²

*Forrest to his superior Confederate General Joseph Wheeler concerning the South's loss at the Battle of Dover, waged February 3, 1863:*
☞ "General Wheeler, I advised against this attack, and said all a subordinate officer should have said against it, and nothing you can now say or do will bring back my brave men lying dead or wounded and freezing around that fort to-night. I mean no disrespect to you; you know my feelings of personal friendship for you; you can have my sword if you demand it; but there is one thing I do want you to put in that report to General Bragg—tell him that I will be in my coffin before I will fight again under your command."⁵³

Dr. James B. Cowan, Forrest's chief surgeon.

*After Confederate Captain Sam L. Freeman, a much beloved heavy set Christian officer, was captured at the Battle of Franklin I on April 10, 1863, he was marched off to prison. Prodded along and beaten from all sides by his pitiless Union captors, the weary Rebel leader began to lag behind, stumbling on the path. He was then ordered to run, an impossible task, as he had once again fallen to the ground exhausted. Instead of helping him to his feet and assisting him along, as required by both international military law and moral ethics, a member of the Fourth U.S. Cavalry rode up to Captain Freeman and shot him in the head at point blank range, killing him instantly.⁵⁴ His body was left unceremoniously on the dusty road where he fell.⁵⁵ When Forrest arrived on the scene his eyes were already filled with tears at the news. Taking Freeman's cold hand, he said:*

☞ "Brave man; none braver!"⁵⁶

Forrest to his superior General John Bell Hood, prior to the Battle of Franklin II, November 30, 1864:
☞ "If you will give me one strong division of infantry with my cavalry, I will agree to flank the Federals from their works within two hours' time."⁵⁷

Forrest's distaste for the art of learning endured throughout his life, both helping and hindering him, even playing a small role in the Confederacy's downfall.⁵⁸ Though outwardly he pretended not to care, he certainly, at times, became defensive about his limited schooling, and often felt uncomfortable around the more educated. He once bristled:
☞ "I never see a pen but what I think of a snake."⁵⁹

When Union General Able D. Streight refused to surrender to Forrest until he knew how many men Forrest had, Forrest answered:
☞ "I've got enough to whip you out of yer boots."⁶⁰

As mentioned, on occasion the General would send unarmed men into battle (his troops were nearly always under-equipped throughout the War).⁶¹ Naturally many balked at the seemingly insane order, at which Forrest barked:
☞ "Get in line and advance on the enemy with the rest! I want to make as big a show as possible!"⁶²

In a field report to Lieutenant Colonel T. M. Jack dated March 21, 1864, Forrest wrote of horrid conditions in his native state at the time:
☞ "The whole of West Tennessee is overrun by bands and squads of robbers, horse thieves and deserters, whose depredations and unlawful appropriations of private property are rapidly and effectually depleting the country."⁶³

The following is an example of Forrest's usual demand to those Yankee commanders who were unfortunate enough to meet him on the battlefield. This one, written out by Forrest on March 25, 1864, was dispatched by courier to Union officer Colonel S. G. Hicks at Paducah, Kentucky:
☞ "Having a force amply sufficient to carry your works and reduce the

place, and in order to avoid the unnecessary effusion of blood, I demand the surrender of the fort and troops, with all public property. If you surrender, you shall be treated as prisoners of war; but if I have to storm your works, you may expect no quarter."[64]

*On April 12, 1864, as Forrest was leading his troops forward to fight what would become known as the Battle of Fort Pillow, he said:*
☞ "Men, do as I say and I will always lead you to victory."[65]

*Forrest to his troops at the Battle of Brice's Cross Roads on June 10, 1864:*
☞ "Get up, men. I have ordered Bell to charge on the left. When you hear his guns, and the bugle sounds, every man must charge, and we will give them hell."[66]

*One of Forrest's favorite commands:*
☞ "Give 'em hell boys!"[67]

*In the fall of 1864, near Pulaski, Tennessee, Forrest and his men found themselves before a blockhouse full of Unions troops. The garrison was led by a truly stubborn Dutch Yankee officer, who refused several of Forrest's polite requests that he surrender. At this point Forrest ran out of patience, yelling to his staff:*
☞ "Does the damned fool want to be blown up? Well, I'll blow him up, then. Give him hell, Captain Morton—as hot as you've got it, too"[68]

*Once, when Forrest asked one of his lieutenants to help their soldiers with some grunt work, the young man refused, using the excuse that he was an officer. At this the General lifted his sword over his head and bellowed:*
☞ "I'll officer *you!*"[69]

Captain Matthew C. Galloway, an aide-de-camp under Forrest.

*To his superior General Gideon Pillow at the Battle of Fort Donelson, fought February 11-16, 1862:*
☞ "We can't hold 'em, but we can run over 'em."[70]

*Once, when one of Union General Cadwallader C. Washburn's staff members confronted Forrest with a "sassy" comment about how they planned on capturing him, Forrest replied:*
☞ "You may tell the general for me, that I am going back on the same road I came by, and if we meet, I promise to whip him out of his boots."[71]

*No Confederate officer was better at enlisting new soldiers than General Forrest. One of his favorite methods was to throw a neighborhood barbeque and invite all of the locals. He also ran advertisements that were calculated to light a fire under even the most passive Southern male, such as this recruitment ad which he placed in a local newspaper:*
☞ "Come on boys, if you want a heap o' fun and to kill some Yankees!"[72]

*Forrest and his command were about to "ride out" of Fort Donelson to avoid capture by the Yanks, when he came across a subordinate, Captain John S. Wilkes. When Forrest invited Wilkes to join him the officer refused, saying that he would prefer staying with those who were about to surrender. To this Forrest replied:*
☞ "All right; I admire your loyalty, but damn your judgment!"[73]

*When Confederate Captain John S. Wilkes rode forty miles to see Forrest trounce the Yanks at the Battle of Harrisburg/Tupelo in July 1864, Forrest snapped at him:*
☞ "Go back captain; this is not my fight; this is General Stephen Dill Lee's battle, and I am not responsible for it."[74]

*Upon hearing that his superiors were planning on surrendering Fort Donelson to Union General Ulysses S. Grant:*
☞ "I did not come here to surrender my command! I would rather my bones bleach on the hillside than go to a Yankee prison!"[75]

*Forrest loved the game of checkers and was an expert player who seldom lost a*

## THE QUOTABLE NATHAN BEDFORD FORREST ~ 37

match. As such, checker references often came up in his speech, as in the following quote concerning the Battle of Okolona, February 22, 1864:
☞ "I saw [Union General Benjamin] Grierson make a 'bad move,' and then I rode right over him."[76]

After the disastrous Battle of Franklin II, November 30, 1864, at which Forrest fought (this area is still known today as "Forrest's Crossing"), he sent a handwritten note to a friend, Laura Galloway of Columbia, Tennessee. It reads:
☞ "My compliments to Miss Laura—hoping she may never have to morn over another defete of the Confederate army. N. B. Forrest, Maj. Genl."[77]

In early 1865 Forrest accurately predicted the end of the Southern Confederacy with these words:

Captain Nathan Boone—a cousin of the author, noted frontiersman Daniel Boone, and contemporary singer/actor Pat Boone—commanded General Forrest's famous Escort.

☞ "To my mind it is evident that the end is not far off; it will only be a question of time as to when General [Robert E.] Lee's lines at Petersburg will be broken, for Grant is wearing him out; with unlimited resources of men and money, he must ultimately force Lee to leave Virginia or surrender. Lee's army will never leave Virginia; they will not follow him out when the time comes, and that will end the war."[78]

During the Battle of Selma, April 2, 1865, Forrest was nearly killed in hand-to-hand combat by a young Yankee officer named Frank White. A few days later, his arm in a sling, Forrest commented on the event:
☞ "If that boy had known enough to give me the point of his saber instead of its edge, I should not have been here to tell you about it."[79]

After General Robert E. Lee's "surrender" at Appomattox on April 9, 1865, a despondent Forrest momentarily considered continuing the fight further South. His mood at the time was encapsulated during a night ride with his aid-de-camp Major Charles W. Anderson. When they came to a fork in the road, Anderson asked, "Which way sir?", to which Forrest replied:

☞ "Either. If one road led to hell and the other to Mexico, I would be indifferent as to which one to take."[80]

After some thought, however, Forrest came to his senses, telling Major Anderson:
☞ "I will share the fate of my men."[81]

Eventually Forrest came to completely accept the destiny of his nation and submitted to the inevitable. When he was prevailed upon by former Tennessee governor Isham G. Harris and Mississippi governor Charles Clark to remain in the field and carry on the War against the North, Forrest replied:

☞ "Men, you may all do as you please, but I'm a-goin' home. Any man who is in favor of a further prosecution of this war is a fit subject for a lunatic asylum, and ought to be sent there immediately."[82]

This old illustration shows the Yanks frantically retreating over Tishomingo Creek under Forrest's overwhelming show of force at the Battle of Brice's Cross Roads on June 10, 1864.

# MILITARY REPORTS AND DISPATCHES

## 1861-1865

*In chronological order*

During Lincoln's War Forrest wrote out dozens of field reports and military dispatches—some formal and dry, others containing fascinating examples of the General's wit, wisdom, and political views. This chapter includes excerpts from, and in some cases the full text of, reports from each year of the conflict.[83]

*Even before Forrest fought in his first battle he was raising hell among the Yankees, on this particular occasion in Kentucky. The following very interesting report, dated December 5, 1861, reveals the fighting spirit of then Colonel Forrest during the first year of Lincoln's War:*

 "Report of Col. N. B. Forrest, Tennessee Cavalry (Confederate). Regimental Headquarters, Hopkinsville, Ky., December 5, 1861. Leaving Hopkinsville November 24 with 300 men and their officers, under orders from brigade headquarters, we went to Greenville, where we found some arms and equipments belonging to the enemy, as will be seen by a list herewith returned; also a [Yankee] soldier in full uniform, whom we made prisoner and returned to the commander of the post; from thence to Madisonville, where I sent Captain Overton, with 30 men, in the direction of Ashbysburg and Calhoun, who reported that all the troops had left the former place and gone to the latter (Calhoun). I then sent a scout to Henderson, dressed as a citizen, who reported that all the Federal forces had been sent from that town to Calhoun and their sick to Evansville.

"I then visited Providence and Claysville and Morganfield, at all of which places the people met us with smiles and cheers, and fed and greeted us kindly.

"I then went to Caseyville, on the Ohio River; then up the Tradewater 12 miles, where I crossed and went to Marion, in Crittenden County. When near that place a lady came from her door and begged in the name of her children for help, and representing that her husband (who was a citizen of standing and unconnected with the war) had been captured by Federal soldiers, led on and assisted by citizens of the neighborhood, whose names being given, I deemed it proper to arrest. William Akers was arrested, and when I approached the house of Jonathan Bells he shot the surgeon of my regiment from the door and escaped by a back opening in the house. A noble and brave man, and skillful surgeon, and high-toned gentleman was Dr. Van Wyck, and his loss was deeply felt by the whole regiment. Dispatching the body in care of Major Kelly [Kelley], with 100 men, to Hopkinsville. I remained in the vicinity of Marion another day, and my scouts arrested one Federal soldier and brought him as prisoner, and killed one Scott, the leader of the band, who had sworn to shoot Southern men from their horses and behind trees, he (Scott) attempting it by wounding three horses with a shot-gun. The scouts found with him

Colonel William L. Duckworth served under Forrest in the Seventh Tennessee Cavalry.

three guns and a pistol, which are returned to the Ordnance Department; also two horses of the enemy.

"From Marion I went to Dycusburg and Eddyville, where I learned that no boats or soldiers had been on the Cumberland for twelve days at those points. The people at the latter places treated us with the utmost liberality and kindness.

"It is believed that the expedition has done great good in giving confidence to the Southern-rights men, destroying the distorted ideas of Union men, who expected every species of abuse at the hands of the Confederate soldiers, many of them expressing their agreeable disappointment and change of views in regard to our army, and not a few assured us that they would no longer use any influence against the cause of the South. Universal kindness was the policy of the officers in command. With me were Captains Overton, May, Fruitt [Trewhitt?], and Hambrick, in command of detachments of their own companies, and Lieutenant Sims, in command of a detachment of Captain Gould's company, and Lieutenant Gentry, in command of a detachment of Captain Logan's company, and as guide Lieutenant Wallace, of Captain G. A. Huwald's company.

"A number of hogs and cattle were started from the counties between this and the river and along the river under the auspices of the expedition.

"There are no Federal forces remaining on this side of the Ohio from the mouth of Green to the mouth of Cumberland, and with the exception of a few scouts none have been there for twelve days.

"After I left Madisonville, Jackson's cavalry visited the place, about 400 in number, but he attempted no pursuit; he might have easily overtaken us. After we were at Caseyville 200 Federal troops came there and captured about eighty hogs, became intoxicated on stolen whisky, and left in a row [fight]. All of which is respectfully submitted. N. B. Forrest, Colonel, Commanding Forrest Regiment Cavalry."[84]

*Forrest's first major engagement took place at the Battle of Sacramento, Kentucky on December 28, 1861. Here is his official report:*
☞ "Report of Col. Nathan B. Forrest, Forrest's Regiment, C. S. Army. Hopkinsville, Ky., December 30, 1861. Under orders to reconnoiter to the front, especially in the direction of Rochester and Greenville, and if

An example of one of Forrest's hundreds of military dispatches, this one dated September 29, 1861, Memphis, Tennessee.

deemed best to continue our observations towards Ramsey, my command left camp Thursday, 26th instant, myself with detachments from Companies A, C, and D, First Lieutenant Crutcher, Captains May and Gould with a detachment of 25 men of Captain Meriwether's company, under his command, Major Kelly [Kelley], with detachments from Companies E, F, and G, under Lieutenants Hampton, Kance, and Cowan, having been ordered to Greenville to await orders. Leaving the Greenville road 4 miles from Hopkinsville I moved in the direction of Rochester, until fully satisfied that there were no movements of the enemy in that direction.

"The next day, on reaching the Russellville and Greenville road, I turned towards Greenville, and on Saturday morning formed a junction with a detachment of 40 cavalry from Russellville, under command of

Lieutenant-Colonel Starnes and Captain McLemore, who, with Major Kelly, were awaiting my arrival at Greenville. Colonel Starnes had the day before been at South Carrollton, where he had engaged a party of the enemy, killing 3.

"Hearing nothing still from the enemy, it was determined to extend our march to the vicinity of Rumsey. The command, about 300 strong, were moved forward in one column, with advance guard under Captain Meriwether and rear under Captain McLemore; the head of the column under my command; the center under Major Kelly, and the rear under Lieutenant-Colonel Starnes. We had moved 8 miles down the Rumsey road when information reached me that the enemy 500 strong had that morning crossed from Calhoun to Rumsey. My men were ordered to a rapid pace, and as the news of the proximity of the enemy ran down the column it was impossible to repress jubilant and defiant shouts, which reached the height of enthusiasm as the women from the houses waved us forward. A beautiful young lady, smiling, with untied tresses floating in the breeze, on horseback, met the column just before our advance guard came up with the rear of the enemy, infusing nerve into my arm and kindling knightly chivalry within my heart.

"One mile this side the village of Sacramento our advance guard came up with their rear guard, who halted, seemingly in doubt whether we were friends or foes. Taking a Maynard rifle, I fired at them, when they rode off rapidly to

Colonel Edmund Winchester Rucker, a close cousin of the author (who descends from the Ruckers of Virginia), headed Rucker's Brigade under Forrest. The colonel fought gallantly alongside his commander throughout the Tennessee Campaign in late 1864, and lost his left arm at the disastrous Battle of Nashville, December 15-16. Rucker and Forrest were good friends and after Lincoln's War, from 1869 to 1874, the two went into the railroad business together. Rucker is the grandson of General James Winchester, a co-founder of the city of Memphis, Tennessee.

their column. The column moved up the hill and formed just over its brow. I ordered up the head of my column, telling my men to hold their fire until within good range. The enemy commenced firing from the time we were within 200 yards of them. When we had moved 120 yards farther I ordered my men to fire. After three rounds I found that my men were not up in sufficient numbers to pursue them with success, and as they showed signs of fight, I ordered the advance to fall back. The enemy at once attempted to flank our left, and moved towards us and appeared greatly animated, supposing we were in retreat. They had moved down over 100 yards and seemed to be forming for a charge, when, the remainder of my men coming up, I dismounted a number of men with Sharp's carbines and Maynard rifles to act as sharpshooters; ordered a flank movement upon the part of Major Kelly and Colonel Starnes upon the right and left, and the detachments from the companies under my command, still mounted, were ordered to charge the enemy's center.

"The men sprang to the charge with a shout, while the undergrowth so impeded the flankers that the enemy, broken by the charge and perceiving the movement on their flanks, broke in utter confusion, and, in spite of the efforts of a few officers, commenced a disorderly flight at full speed, in which the officers soon joined. We pressed closely on their rear, only getting an occasional shot, until we reached the village of Sacramento, when, the best mounted men of my companies coming up, there commenced a promiscuous saber slaughter of their rear, which was continued at almost full speed for 2 miles beyond the village, leaving their bleeding and wounded strewn along the whole route. At this point Captain Bacon, and but a little before Captain Burges, were run through with saber thrusts, and Captain Davis thrown from his horse and surrendered as my prisoner, his shoulder being dislocated by the fall. The enemy, without officers, threw down their arms and depended alone upon the speed of their horses. Those of my men whose horses were able to keep up found no difficulty in piercing through every one they came up with, but as my horses were almost run down while theirs were much fresher, I deemed it best to call off the chase, for such it had become, leaving many wounded men hanging to their saddles to prevent their falling from their horses. Returning, we found their dead and wounded in every direction. Those who were able

Brigadier General Tyree H. Bell commanded Bell's Brigade in Forrest' Cavalry.

to be moved we placed in wagons. Captains Bacon and Burges were made as comfortable as we could, and applied to the nearest farm house to take care of them.

"There were killed on the field and mortally wounded, who have since died, about 65; wounded and taken prisoners, about 35, making their loss about 100. Among their killed were two captains and three lieutenants and several non-commissioned officers.

"The fight occurred in the woods; the run was principally along lanes. I have the pleasure of stating that Colonel Starnes and Major Kelly acted in the most noble and chivalrous manner, and, indeed, I can say that Captain Gould, Captain May, Captain Meriwether (who unfortunately fell in front of the engagement), Lieutenant Crutcher, in command of Captain Overton's company; Lieutenant Nance left in command of Captain Hambrick's company; Lieutenant Cowan, in command of Captain Logan's company (he acting as surgeon at the time), and Lieutenant Hampton, in command of Captain Truett's [?] company, with the men under their respective commands are deserving praise for their conduct.

"Our loss was Captain Meriwether and Private Terry, of Captain McLemore's company, killed, and 3 privates slightly wounded; 2 from Captain May's and the other from Captain Hambrick's.

"We returned to Greenville the night of the fight (Saturday), and from thence started to camp, and arrived last night.

"Before closing this report I most respectfully call your attention to the gallant conduct of Lieutenant Bailey, of Captain Gould's company; Private J. W. Ripley, of Captain May's company, and Private J. M. Luxton, also of Captain May's; and Private B. W. Johnson, of Captain Logan's company, and, indeed, many others, whose horses being not quite so fast, did not come immediately under my own observation.

Capt. M. B. Logan (who was acting as surgeon on that occasion) deserves praise for his noble conduct throughout the engagement.

"All of which is most respectfully submitted. Respectfully, N. B. Forrest, Colonel, Commanding Forrest Regiment."[85]

*Forrest's next conflict of consequence was the Battle of Fort Donelson, which took place February 11-16, 1862. What follows is Forrest's official report of the conflict:*

☞ "Reports of Col. Nathan B. Forrest, Tennessee Cavalry. February —, 1862. Having been ordered by Brigadier-General Clark to Fort Donelson from Hopkinsville, I arrived at Fort Donelson on Monday evening, February 10, and finished crossing with my command on Tuesday morning.

"On the same afternoon I was ordered, with 300 of my cavalry, to reconnoiter in the direction of Fort Henry. We met about 3 miles from Fort Donelson the enemy's cavalry, supposed to be about 600, and, after a short skirmish, pressing them hard about 6 miles, captured 1 prisoner and mortally wounded several others.

"The following morning I was ordered out with my own regiment, three Kentucky companies, viz, Captains Williams, Wilcox, and Hewey's, and Lieutenant-Colonel Gantt's battalion of Tennessee cavalry (the commanding general having signified to me the night before his desire that I should take charge of all the cavalry at the post as brigadier of cavalry.)

"I had gone about 2 miles on the road towards Fort Henry when we met the advance of the enemy. My advance guard engaged them, when I sent forward three rifle companies, and after a skirmish they retreated, leaving several dead and wounded. The enemy halted, and, after maneuvering for some time, commenced to move by a parallel road towards the fort. Receiving information of this change, I changed my position from the right to the extreme left of my line of battle, throwing two squadrons of cavalry across the road. As soon as the enemy's advance came in sight I again attacked them vigorously. The enemy were on an elevated ridge, thickly wooded, and, when the attack was made, little else than their cavalry could be seen.

"My first squadron as skirmishers, having been dismounted,

were hotly engaged with greatly superior numbers. To enable them to withdraw, the second squadron was ordered to charge, hearing which, Major Kelly, by my request, commanding the left (now center) of my line, ordered an advance of the three squadrons under his command. The enemy gave back at the point where the charge was made, and the cavalry wheeling out of the way on their flank opposite Major Kelly, the infantry rose from the ground and poured in at short range a terrific fire of musketry, accompanied by a volley of grape. I was now able to mount and draw off in good order my skirmishers, and, finding the enemy in large force, ordered my cavalry to fall back, no infantry being near to support me. In answer to my couriers from the fort, General Buckner (General G. J. Pillow absent at Cumberland City) now ordered me back within our intrenchments.

Colonel Robert McCulloch served under General Forrest as a brigade commander in the Second Missouri Cavalry.

"This skirmish was from about 9 a. m. to near 2 p. m. We killed during the day a hundred men and wounded several hundred more, which so delayed the advance of the enemy that they did not move to the attack that day, satisfying themselves with planting a few cannon and commencing at long range a slow cannonade.

"In the afternoon General Floyd reached the fort, and the whole army, infantry and cavalry, were engaged during the night in throwing up intrenchments, crowning several hills surrounding Dover. The enemy planted their batteries during the night, and commenced a cannonade from their batteries and ten gunboats early on the morning of Thursday. Soon after, our intrenchments were vigorously attacked at all points, and for six hours there was scarcely a cessation of small-arms and artillery. The musketry ceased about 1 p. m., the cannonading continuing until after dark. The gunboats drew off early in the engagement, supposed to be crippled, returning occasionally. The cavalry were but little engaged, acting only as pickets and couriers.

"On Friday I was ordered out with the infantry, passing our intrenchments on the left; but after maneuvering a short time and some sharp shooting between the cavalry and the enemy, I was ordered back into the intrenchments. A demand was then made on me for sharpshooters to dislodge the enemy, who were from heights and trees annoying our infantry in the intrenchments, which we accomplished in about two hours, returning to my command about the time the gunboat attack was made on the fort. Of this attack I was an eye-witness, and have never seen a description which did anything like justice to the attack or defense. More determination could not have been exhibited by the attacking party, while more coolness and bravery never was manifested than was seen in our artillerists. Never was there greater anxiety depicted in the face of brave men than during the terrific roar of cannon, relieved ever and anon by the slow but regular report of our one single 10-inch gun. Never were men more jubilant than when the victory crowned the steady bravery of our little fort; old men wept; shout after shout went up; the gunboats driven back; the army was in the best possible spirits, feeling that, relieved of their greatest terror, they could whip any land force that could be brought against them.

"During the night I was called into council with the generals commanding, when it was determined to bring on the attack the next morning by again passing our intrenchments and attacking the enemy's right.

"In the early gray of the morning I moved to the attack, the cavalry on the left and in the advance. I found the enemy prepared to receive us, and were again engaged with the sharpshooters till our infantry were formed for the attack, the first gun from the enemy killing a horse in my regiment. General B. H. Johnson commanded the left, which now moved to the front. An obstinate fight of two hours ended in the retreat of the enemy. The undergrowth was so thick that I could scarcely press my horses through it. Finding that the flank of the enemy in retreat was exposed across an open field to my front and left, I immediately led my cavalry to the field, but found the ground a marsh, and we were unable to pass it.

"The enemy formed in the edge of a second field to our front and right, and flanking the left of our advancing line of infantry. We could not move to flank them, but by maneuvering to their front and right doubtless prevented their attempting a flank movement on our infantry. Finding that our advancing line of infantry would cut them off while the cavalry prevented their flanking us, they commenced a retreat, accompanied by their cavalry, which we could now see in the distance, but not participating during the day in the fight. Our infantry had now driven them near a mile, they doggedly disputing the whole ground, leaving dead and wounded scattered through the woods and fields up in the ravine. The enemy, leaving their third position for the first time, retreated in haste, advancing by a road through a ravine. I here passed our line of infantry with my command in moving to the center.

Captain H. A. Tyler served under Forrest in Company A, Twelfth Kentucky Cavalry.

"I charged the enemy's battery of six guns, which had kept several of our regiments in check for several hours, killing and slaughtering a great many of our men. I captured the battery, killing most of the men and horses. I then immediately moved on the flank of the enemy, obstinately maintaining their position. They finally gave way, our infantry and cavalry both charging them at the same time, committing great slaughter. Moving still farther to our right, I found a regiment of our infantry in confusion, which I relieved by charging the enemy to their front. Here 64 of the enemy were found in 40 yards square. General Pillow, coming up, ordered me to charge the enemy in a ravine. I charged by squadrons, filing the first company of each squadron to the right, and the second to the left, on reaching the ravine, firing and falling in the rear of the third squadron until the three squadrons had charged. We here completely routed the enemy, leaving some 200 dead in the hollow, accomplishing what three different regiments had failed to do. Seeing the enemy's battery to our right about to turn on us, I now ordered a charge on this battery, from which we drove the enemy, capturing two guns. Following down the ravine captured the third, which they were endeavoring to carry off, gunners and drivers retreating up the hill. In this charge I killed about 50 sharpshooters, who were supporting the guns. I ordered forward a number of scouts, who, returning, informed me that the enemy, with three guns and three regiments of infantry, were moving up by the road from Fort Henry. We had driven the enemy back without a reverse from the left of our intrenchments to the center, having opened three different roads by which we might have retired if the generals had, as was deemed best in the council the night before, ordered the retreat of the army. Informing General Pillow of the position the enemy had taken, he ordered two new regiments and one of the regiments in the field, with one piece of artillery, to attack the enemy.

"The fight here ended about 2.30 p. m. without any change in our relative positions. We were employed the remainder of the evening in gathering up the arms, and assisting in getting off the wounded. I was three times over the battle-field, and late in the evening was 2 miles up the river on the road to the forge. There were none of the enemy in sight when dark came on. Saturday night our troops slept, flushed with victory, and confident they could drive the enemy back to the Tennessee River the next morning.

"About 12 o'clock at night I was called in council with the generals, who had under discussion the surrender of the fort. They reported that the enemy had received 11,000 re-enforcements since the fight. They supposed the enemy had returned to the positions they had occupied the day before.

"I returned to my quarters and sent out two men, who, going by a road up the bank of the river, returned without seeing any of the enemy, only fires, which I believed to be the old camp fires, and so stated to the generals; the wind, being very high, had fanned them into a blaze.

"When I returned General Buckner declared that he could not hold his position. Generals Floyd and Pillow gave up the responsibility of the command to him, and I told them that I neither could nor would surrender my command. General Pillow then said I could cut my way out if I chose to do so, and he and General Floyd agreed to come out with me. I got my command ready and reported at headquarters. General Floyd informed me that General Pillow had left, and that he would go by boat.

"I moved out by the road we had gone out the morning before. When about a mile out crossed a deep slough from the river, saddle-skirt deep, and filed into the road to Cumberland Iron Works. I ordered Major Kelly and Adjutant Schuyler to remain at the point where we entered this road with one company, where the enemy's cavalry would attack if they attempted to follow us. They remained until day was dawning. Over 500 cavalry had passed, a company of artillery horses had followed, and a number of men from different regiments, passing over hard-frozen ground. More than two hours had been occupied in passing. Not a gun had been fired at us. Not an enemy had been seen or heard.

"The enemy could not have reinvested their former position without traveling a considerable distance and camped upon the dead and dying, as there had been great slaughter upon that portion of the field, and I am clearly of the opinion that two-thirds of our army could have marched out without loss, and that, had we continued the fight the next day, we should have gained a glorious victory, as our troops were in fine spirits, believing we had whipped them, and the roads through which we came were open [i.e., no Federal soldiers] as late as 8 o'clock Sunday morning [the 16th], as many of my men, who came out afterwards, report.

Major Charles W. Anderson was one of Forrest's closest confidants during Lincoln's War, serving as both assistant adjutant and inspector general. He wrote out many of Forrest's field reports, the General dictating to him amid the sound of booming cannon.

"I made a slow march with my exhausted horses to Nashville, Tenn., where we arrived on Tuesday morning [the 18th], and reported myself to

General Floyd, who placed me in command of the city on Thursday, at the time of his leaving. I remained in the city until Sunday evening, during which time I was busily engaged with my regiment restoring order to the city and removing public property.

"My loss at the battle in killed, wounded, and taken prisoners amounted to between 300 and 400 men. Among the number was Capt. Charles May, who fell at the head of his company while leading a charge.

"My regiment charged two batteries, taking nine pieces of artillery, which, with near 4,000 stands of arms, I had taken inside of our lines. I cannot speak too highly of the gallant manner in which my officers and men conducted themselves on that occasion, as well as others that came under my observation, with the exception of Lieutenant-Colonel Gantt, commanding a battalion of Tennessee Cavalry, who failed to fight on Saturday, and refused to bring his men out with my regiment on Sunday morning when ordered to do so.

"Respectfully submitted. N. B. Forrest, Colonel, Commanding Forrest's Regiment of Cavalry."[86]

*The loss of Fort Donelson greatly upset the balance of military power in the region (in favor of the Yanks), spreading fear and panic throughout the Southern citizenry. One result was a riot in Nashville that lasted for several days, February 16-18, 1862. Forrest happened to be in the city at the time and masterfully quelled the disorder, peacefully evacuating most of the town. On March 22, 1862, Forrest gave the following "response" to "interrogatories of Committee of Confederate House of Representatives" concerning the situation:*

☞ "Interrogatory 1st. I was not at the city of Nashville at the time of its surrender, but was there at the time the enemy made their entrance into that part of the city known as Edgefield, having left Fort Donelson, with my command, on the morning of its surrender, and reached Nashville on Tuesday, February 18, about 10 a.m. I remained in the city up to the Sunday evening following.

"Interrogatory 2d. It would be impossible to state, from the data before me, the value of the stores either in the Quartermaster's or Commissary Departments, having no papers then nor any previous knowledge of the stores. The stores in the Quartermaster's Department consisted of all stores necessary to the department—clothing especially, in large amounts, shoes, harness, etc., with considerable unmanufactured

A map of the Battle of Brice's Cross Roads, which many consider to be Forrest's greatest victory.

material. The commissary stores were meat, flour, sugar, molasses, and coffee. There was a very large amount of meat in store and on the landing at my arrival, though large amounts had already been carried away by citizens.

"Interrogatory 3d. A portion of these stores had been removed before the surrender. A considerable amount of meat on the landing, I was informed, was thrown into the river on Sunday before my arrival and carried off by the citizens. The doors of the commissary depot were thrown open, and the citizens in dense crowds were packing and hauling off the balance at the time of my arrival on Tuesday. The quartermaster's stores were also open, and the citizens were invited to come and help themselves, which they did in larger crowds, if possible, than at the other department.

"Interrogatories 4th and 5th. On Tuesday morning I was ordered by General Floyd to take command of the city, and attempted to drive the mob from the doors of the departments, which mob was composed of straggling soldiers and citizens of all grades. The mob had taken possession of the city to that extent that every species of property was unsafe. Houses were closed, carriages and wagons were concealed to prevent the mob from taking possession of them. Houses were being seized everywhere. I had to call out my cavalry, and, after every other means failed, charge the mob before I could get it so dispersed as to get wagons to the doors of the departments to load up the stores for transportation. After the mob was partially dispersed and quiet restored a number of citizens furnished wagons and assisted in loading them. I was busily engaged in this work on Friday, Saturday, and Sunday. I transported 700 hundred large boxes of clothing to the Nashville and Chattanooga Railroad depot, several hundred bales of osnaburgs and other military goods from the Quartermaster's Department, most, if not all, of the shoes having been seized by the mob. I removed about 700 or 800 wagon loads of meat. The high water having destroyed the bridges so as to stop the transportation over the Nashville and Chattanooga Railroad, I had large amounts of this meat taken over the Tennessee and Alabama Railroad. By examination on Sunday morning I found a large amount of fixed ammunition in the shape of cartridges and ammunition for light artillery in the magazine, which, with the assistance of General Harding, I conveyed over 7 miles on the Tennessee and Alabama Railroad in wagons, to the amount of 30 odd wagon loads, after the enemy had reached the river. A portion was sent on to Murfreesborough in wagons. The quartermaster's stores which had not already fallen into the hands of the mob were all removed, save a lot of rope, loose shoes, and a large number of tents. The mob had already possessed themselves of a large amount of these stores. A large quantity of meat was left in store and on the river bank and some at the Nashville and Chattanooga Railroad depot, on account of the break in the railroad. I cannot estimate the amount, as several store-houses had not been opened up to the time of my leaving. All stores left fell into the hands of the enemy, except forty pieces of light artillery, which were burned and spiked by order of General Floyd, as were the guns at Fort Zollicoffer. My proposition to remove these stores, made by telegraph to Murfreesborough, had the sanction of General A. S. Johnston.

"Interrogatory 6th. No effort was made, save by the mob, who were endeavoring to possess themselves of these stores, to prevent their removal, and a very large amount was taken off before I was placed in command of the city.

"Interrogatory 7th. It was eight days from the time the quartermaster left the city before the arrival of the enemy, commissaries and other persons connected with these departments leaving at the same time. With proper diligence on their part I have no doubt all the public stores might have been transported to places of safety.

"Interrogatory 8th. Up to Saturday the railroads were open and might have been used to transport these stores. Saturday the bridges of the Nashville and Chattanooga Railroad gave way. Besides these modes of conveyance, a large number of wagons might have been obtained, had the quiet and the order of the city been maintained, and large additional amounts of stores might by these means have been transported to places of safety.

"Interrogatories 9th and 10th. I saw no officer connected with the Quartermaster's or Commissary Departments except Mr. Patton, who left on Friday. I did not at any time meet or hear of Maj. V. K. Stevenson in the city during my stay there.

"Interrogatories 11th, 12th, and 13th. From my personal knowledge I can say nothing of the manner in which Major Stevenson left the city. Common rumor and many reliable citizens informed me that Major Stevenson left by a special train Sunday evening, February 16, taking personal baggage, furniture, carriage, and carriage-horses, the train ordered by himself, as president of the railroad.

"Interrogatory 14th. All the means of transportation were actually necessary for the transportation of Government stores and sick and wounded soldiers, many of whom fell into the hands of the enemy for want of it, and might have been saved by the proper use of the means at hand. The necessity for these means of transportation for stores will be seen by the above answers which I have given. I have been compelled to be as brief as possible in making the above answers, my whole time being engaged, as we seem to be upon the eve of another great battle. The city was in a much worse condition than I can convey an idea of on paper, and the loss of public stores must be estimated by millions of dollars. The panic was entirely useless and not at all justified by the

A portrait of some of Forrest's foremost enemies: Union cavalrymen.

circumstances. General Harding and the mayor of the city, with Mr. Williams, deserve special mention for assistance rendered in removing the public property. In my judgment, if the quartermaster and commissary had remained at their post and worked diligently with the means at their command, the Government stores might all have been saved between the time of the fall of Fort Donelson and the arrival of the enemy at Nashville. Respectfully submitted. N. B. Forrest, Colonel, Commanding Forrest's Brigade of Cavalry."[87]

*On July 13, 1862, Forrest raided and successfully captured Murfreesboro, Tennessee. It was his forty-first birthday, so he had two reasons to celebrate that day. Here is his official report of the engagement:*

"☞ We left Chattanooga on July 9 with the Texan Rangers, under Colonel Wharton, and the Second Georgia Cavalry, under Colonel Lawton. We made a forced march of nearly 50 miles, reaching Altamont on the night of the 10th instant. After resting one night we passed on to McMinnville, where I was joined on the night of the 11th by Colonel Morrison with a portion of the First Georgia Cavalry, two companies of Colonel Spiller's battalion, under Major Smith, and two companies of Kentuckians, under Captains Taylor and Waltham. After this junction my whole force was about 1,400 men, and both men and horses were much jaded and worn by their long travel. After feeding and refreshing for a single day and being joined by some few volunteers I left on the 12th at 1 o'clock for Murfreesborough. It was over 50 miles to our destination, but there was no halt except for a short time to feed the men and horses.

"We approached Murfreesborough about 4.30 A.M. and fortunately captured the pickets of the enemy without firing a gun. I then learned that there were two regiments in and near Murfreesborough, one the Ninth Michigan and the other the Third Minnesota, 200 Pennsylvania cavalry, 100 of the Eighth Kentucky, and Captain Hewett's battery of four guns, numbering in all 1,400 or 1,500 men, under the command of General Thomas Crittenden, of Indiana. There were said to be two camps, one in Murfreesborough of one infantry regiment and the cavalry, the other with the artillery about a mile distant, and a small force with the officers in the court-house and private houses around the public square. I decided immediately to attack the camp in town and the buildings, while the camp with the artillery should be held in check until the first was stormed and surrendered. Colonel Wharton with his Texan Rangers was ordered to charge the camp in town. He moved forward in gallant style at the head of his men, but owing to the urgent necessity of using a portion of the Rangers for the attack on the buildings he did not carry with him but two of his companies. This fact, however, did not abate his courage or that of his men. They charged over the tent ropes right into the camp. Colonel Wharton was soon severely wounded and the command of his Rangers devolved on Colonel Walker.

"Colonel Morrison with a portion of the Second Georgia was ordered to storm the court-house while the balance of the Texan Rangers were attacking the private buildings. After two or three hours hard struggle the court-house was fired and surrendered to Colonel

Morrison. The private buildings were also cleared by the Rangers and General Crittenden and his staff surrendered.

"Lieut. Col. [Arthur] Hood, of the Second Georgia, with a portion of his force was ordered to storm the jail, which he did, releasing many prisoners confined for political offenses; he also took the telegraph office, capturing the operator.

"Colonel Lawton, with the First Georgia, the Tennesseeans and Kentuckians, was ordered to attack the second camp with the artillery, which he did with great efficiency for several hours. The Tennesseeans, under Major Smith, and Kentuckians, under Captains Taylor and Waltham, stood the fire of shot and shell like veterans. The Georgians, under Captain Dunlop and Major Harper, made a gallant charge almost to the mouths of the cannon. After fighting them in front two or three hours I took immediate command of this force and charged the rear of the enemy into their camps and burned their camps and stores, demoralizing their force and weakening their strength.

"The force of Texan Rangers sent to attack the first camp was so small that, although they fought with desperate courage and great skill, they were gradually driven back.

"After the court-house and private buildings were surrendered and the fight had lasted five or six hours I prepared my whole force to storm both camps and summoned them to surrender. After some parley Colonel Duffield surrendered the infantry and artillery.

"My aide, Colonel Saunders, rendered me efficient aid until he was severely wounded by a ball from the court-house. Major Strange, my adjutant, also performed his whole duty. Lieutenant-Colonel Walker and Major Harrison, of the

A postwar photo of Captain John C. Jackson, who served in Forrest's Escort.

Civil War cavalrymen, both South and North, were a breed apart. Justly proud of their occupation, this unique assemblage of men was always greeted with special love and respect by local townsfolk.

Rangers, acted with their usual daring and bravery. All the officers and men who acted bravely cannot be particularly mentioned, but they acted their part nobly.

"After the action was over I detached Major Smith to burn a railroad bridge below Murfreesborough, which he executed well. I intended to burn a railroad bridge above Murfreesborough and gave orders for the purpose, but by mistake they were not executed. I had the telegraph wire cut and a large portion of the railroad track torn up. I found four car-loads of provisions on the railroad track and the depot house full of stores, all of which I burned.

"There were between 1,100 and 1,200 privates and non-commissioned officers captured and brought to McMinnville and paroled on condition not to serve until exchanged. The officers have been already sent to Knoxville, in charge of Colonel Wharton (and I trust have safely reached their destination), except one or two who were wounded and left at Murfreesborough, on condition to surrender when restored to health.

"I captured four pieces of artillery—three brass pieces and one Parrott gun—which are still in my possession, with harness and ammunition. There were some 50 or 60 large road wagons with the mule teams, harness, etc., captured. I burnt some of the wagons, which could not be got away, and sent you the balance. There were a large number of cavalry horses, saddles, and small-arms, with the ammunition, captured, and such as I have not been compelled to use are also forwarded to you.

"In consequence of our being compelled to leave Murfreesborough, and not having received reports of the killed from some of my command, it is impossible to report accurately my loss. My best information is that we had about 25 killed and from 40 to 60 wounded. Among those killed is Lieutenant Green, of the Tennessee Battalion. The reports of the officers under my command when furnished will show more definitely the loss.

"The enemy lost about 75 killed and 125 wounded. The pecuniary loss to the enemy must be near half a million of dollars [about $12 million in today's currency]. Yours, respectfully, N. B. Forrest, Brigadier- General, Commanding Brigade of Cavalry."[88]

*In his official report regarding the Battle of Thompson's Station on March 5, 1863, Forrest wrote:*
☞ "No one can regret more than I do the loss of Lieutenant-Colonel Trezevant, commanding Cox's regiment of cavalry, Capt. M. Little, of my escort, and Captain [A. A.] Dysart, of the Third Tennessee Cavalry. They were gallant men, and fell with their faces to the foe. I cannot speak in too high terms of the conduct of my whole command. The colonels commanding led their regiments in person, and it affords me much pleasure to say that officers and men performed their duty well. I discerned no straggling or shirking from duty on the field. Every order was promptly obeyed, and the bravery of the troops alike creditable to them and gratifying to their commanders."[89]

*On August 9, 1863, Forrest, anticipating problems with his superior, the cranky Braxton Bragg, wrote a letter to Confederate General Samuel Cooper at Richmond, asking for an independent command in West Tennessee or Mississippi. Included in Forrest's missive was a proposal for what was certainly the most outstanding plan by a Confederate officer during the entire conflict: prolong the War—thus exhausting the North—by closing down the Yankees' major supply routes, the Mississippi and Tennessee Rivers.[90] By this time most of the Union forces, including those under Grant, were relying strictly on these two waterways for provisions. Had Forrest's proposition (already backed by other important Confederate leaders, such as General Joseph E. Johnston) been taken seriously and implemented, it is clear that the outcome of Lincoln's War would have been very different.[91] Forrest's original letter to Cooper, which, unfortunately, was to pass through Bragg's hands,[92] reads:*
☞ "Headquarters First Division Cavalry, Kingston, August 9, 1863.

General S. Cooper, Adjutant-General, Richmond, Va.:
General,—Prompted by the repeated solicitations of numerous friends and acquaintances resident in west Tennessee and northern Mississippi, also by a desire to serve my country to the best of my ability, and wherever those services can be rendered most available and effective, I respectfully lay before you a proposition which, if approved, will seriously, if not entirely, obstruct the navigation of the Mississippi River, and in sixty days procure a large force now inside the enemy's lines, which without this, or a similar move, cannot be obtained.

"The proposition is this: Give me the command of the forces from Vicksburg to Cairo, or, in other words, all the forces I may collect together and organize between those points—say in northern Mississippi, west Tennessee, and those that may join me from Arkansas, Mississippi, and southern Kentucky. I desire to take with me only about four hundred men from my present command—viz., my escort, sixty; McDonald's battalion, one hundred and fifty; the Second Kentucky Cavalry, two hundred and fifty—selected entirely on account of their knowledge of the country in which I propose to operate. In all, say, men and outfit, four hundred men, with long-range guns (Enfield), four three-inch Dahlgren or Parrott guns, with eight number one horses to each gun and caisson, two wagons for the battery, one pack-mule to every ten men, and two hundred rounds of ammunition for small arms and artillery.

Brigadier General Hylan B. Lyon commanded the Kentucky Brigade of Forrest's Cavalry.

"I would like to have Captain (W. W.) Carnes, now at Chattanooga, in some portion of General Bragg's army, to command the battery, and, in case he was detached for the expedition, that he be allowed to select his cannoneers, etc. I have resided on the Mississippi for over twenty years, was for many years engaged in buying and selling negroes, and know the country perfectly well between Memphis and Vicksburg, and also am well acquainted with all the prominent planters in that region, as well as above Memphis. I also have officers in my command and on my staff who have rafted timber out of the bottoms, and know every foot of the ground between Commerce and Vicksburg. With the force proposed, and my knowledge of the river-bottoms, as well as the knowledge my men have of the country from Vicksburg up, I am confident we could so move and harass and destroy boats on the river that only boats heavily protected by gunboats would be able to make the passage.

"I ask also authority to organize all troops that can be obtained, and that I be promised long-range guns for them as soon as organizations are reported. There are many half-organized regiments, battalions, and companies in northern Mississippi and west Tennessee, but they are without arms and have no way of getting out, and it only requires a little time and a nucleus around which they can form, to organize and put them in the field. I believe that in sixty days I can raise from five to ten thousand men between Vicksburg and Cairo, well mounted and ready for service as soon as provided with guns and ammunition.

"In making this proposition, I desire to state that I do so entirely for the good of the service. I believe that I can accomplish all that I propose to do. I have never asked for position, have taken position and performed the duties assigned me, and have never yet suffered my command to be surprised or defeated. I should leave this department with many regrets, as I am well pleased with the officers in my command and with the division serving under me. I shall especially regret parting with my old brigade. It was organized by me, and a record of its past services and present condition will compare favorably with any cavalry command in the service, and nothing but a desire to destroy the enemy's transports and property, and increase the strength of our army, could for a moment induce me voluntarily to part with them. There are thousands of men where I propose to go that I am satisfied will join me, and that rapidly (otherwise they will remain where they are), until all the country bordering on the Mississippi from Cairo down is taken and permanently occupied by our forces. I am, general, very respectfully, your obedient servant, N. B. Forrest, Brigadier-General."[93]

# THE QUOTABLE NATHAN BEDFORD FORREST  63

*What follows is Forrest's official report on the Battle of Okolona, February 22, 1864, at which, tragically, his favorite (and youngest) brother Jeffrey was killed:*

☞ "Ten miles from Pontotoc they [the Yanks] made a last and final effort to check pursuit, and from their preparations, numbers, and advantageous position no doubt indulged the hope of success. They had formed in three lines across a large field on the left of the road, but which a turn in the road made it directly in our front. Their lines were at intervals of several hundred paces, and the rear and second lines longer than the first. As the advance of my column moved up they opened on us with artillery. My ammunition was nearly exhausted, and I knew that if we faltered they would in turn become the attacking party, and that disaster might follow. Many of my men were broken down and exhausted with clambering the hills on foot and fighting almost constantly for the last 9 miles. I determined, therefore, relying upon the bravery and courage of the few men I had up, to advance to the attack. As we moved up, the whole force charged down at a gallop, and I am proud to say that my men did not disappoint me. Standing firm, they repulsed the grandest cavalry charge I ever witnessed. The Second and Seventh Tennessee drove back the advance line, and as it wheeled in retreat poured upon them a destructive fire. Each successive line of the enemy shared the same fate and fled the field in dismay and confusion, and losing another piece of artillery, and leaving it strewn with dead and wounded men and horses.

"Half of my command were out of ammunition, the men and horses exhausted and worn down with two days' hard riding and fighting, night was at hand, and further pursuit impossible.

"Major-General [Samuel J.] Gholson arrived during the night. His command was small,

Captain John Watson Morton, General Forrest's chief of artillery. After Lincoln's War Morton wrote a book entitled, *The Artillery of Nathan Bedford Forrest's Cavalry*. The author is cousins with Morton's wife, Ellen Bourne Tynes.

but comparatively fresh. I ordered him to follow on the next morning and press them across the Tallahatchie. Having received no official report from him, I cannot give any details of his pursuit after them.

"Considering the disparity in numbers and equipments, I regard the defeat of this force, consisting as it did of the best cavalry in the Federal army, as a victory of which all engaged in it may justly feel proud. It has given, for a time at least, peace and security to a large scope of rich country whose inhabitants anticipated and expected to be overrun, devastated and laid waste, and its moral effect upon the raw, undisciplined and undrilled troops of this command is in value incalculable. It has inspired them with courage and given them confidence in themselves and their commanders. Although many of them were but recently organized, they fought with a courage and daring worthy of veterans.

"I herewith transmit you a list of casualties, which, under all the circumstances, is small, and especially so when compared with that of the enemy.

"The killed and wounded of the enemy who fell into our hands amounts to over 100. We captured 6 pieces of artillery, 3 stand of colors, and 162 prisoners. By pressing every horse, buggy, carriage, and vehicle along the road they were enabled to take off all their wounded, except those severely or mortally wounded, and it is but reasonable to suppose amid a low estimate to place their loss in killed, wounded, and missing at 800.

"My force in the fight did not exceed 2,500 men, while that of the enemy was twenty-seven regiments of cavalry and mounted infantry, estimated at 7,000 strong.

"I regret the loss of some gallant officers. The loss of my brother, Col. J. E. Forrest, is deeply felt by his brigade as well as myself, and it is but just to say that for sobriety, ability, prudence, and bravery he had no superior of his age. Lieutenant-Colonel Barksdale was also a brave and gallant man, and his loss fell heavily on the regiment he commanded, as it was left now without a field officer.

"I desire to testify my appreciation of the skill and ability of Colonels McCulloch, Russell, and Duckworth, commanding brigades. Colonel McCulloch, although wounded on the evening of the 22d, continued in command. Colonel Russell assumed command of Bell's brigade after the injury to Colonel Barteau, and Colonel Duckworth took command of Forrest's brigade after Colonel Forrest fell on the morning of the 22d ultimo.

"I have formally congratulated and returned my thanks to the officers and troops of my command for their gallant and meritorious conduct; for their energy, endurance, and courage, and it would afford me pleasure to mention individual instances of daring and dash which came under my own observation but for fear of doing apparent injustice to others who in other parts of the field perhaps did as well.

Brigadier General Abe Buford commanded a division of Forrest's Cavalry.

"My escort deserves especial mention: Commanded by Lieut. Thomas S. Tate on the 21$^{st}$, and by its commander, Captain Jackson, on the 22d, its battle-flag was foremost in the fray, sustaining its reputation as one of the best fighting cavalry companies in the service. I also desire to acknowledge, as I have often done before, my indebtedness to Maj. J. P. Strange, my assistant adjutant-general; Capt. Charles W. Anderson, my aide-de-camp, and Lieutenant Tate, assistant inspector-general, for prompt and faithful services rendered in the delivery and execution of all my orders on the field. All of which is respectfully submitted. N. B. Forrest, Major-General."[94]

*In an attempt to belittle the South and tarnish Forrest's reputation, Union General Ulysses S. Grant tried to suppress the facts about Forrest's magnificent win at the Battle of Okolona.[95] On March 11, 1864, however, Forrest himself issued the following circular to his men, immortalizing the truth:*

☞ "Columbus, March 11, 1864. The major-general commanding desires to return his thanks and acknowledgments to the officers and men of his command for their recent gallant and meritorious conduct in defeating and routing the largest, most carefully selected, and best equipped cavalry and mounted infantry command ever sent into the field by the enemy. And it affords him both pleasure and pride to say that by your ability, unflinching bravery, and endurance, a force three times your own was defeated, routed, demoralized, and driven from the country, his plans frustrated, his ends unaccomplished, and his forces cut to pieces. Thus by your valor and courage you have given safety and security to the homes and firesides of the defenseless and helpless inhabitants of the country, whose grateful acknowledgments are showered upon you and whose prayers daily and nightly ascend to heaven for your future prosperity and success.

"The major-general commanding deplores the loss of some of his bravest officers and men. They have fallen in the discharge of their duty as soldiers and patriots, and have yielded up their lives in defense of all that man holds dear. He desires that you cherish their memory, emulate their example, and achieve your independence or perish in the attempt.

"In conclusion, the major-general commanding desires to say that all who were engaged may feel justly proud of their participation in a victory so pregnant with disaster to the enemy and so glorious in its results to our cause, and which has delivered a grateful people from that oppression, devastation, and destruction which follows the footsteps of a dastardly and brutal foe.

"By your past conduct and heroism he confidently relies upon and predicts your future success in whipping the enemy wherever you meet them. By command of Major-General Forrest: J. P. Strange, Assistant Adjutant-General."[96]

*Forrest wrote out the following dispatch to Confederate Lieutenant Colonel Thomas M. Jack on March 21, 1864:*

☞ "I forward, for the information of the lieutenant-general commanding, the inclosed statement [below] of outrages committed by the commands of [Union] Col. Fielding Hurst and others of the Federal Army. I desire, if it meets with the approval of the lieutenant-general commanding, that this report may be sent to some newspaper for publication. Such conduct should be made known to the world. Very respectfully, colonel, your obedient servant N. B. Forrest, Major-General, Commanding.

"Hdqrs. Cav. Dept. Of West Tenn. and north Miss., Jackson, March 21, 1864. Lieut. Col. T. M. Jack, Assistant Adjutant-General:

A typical Civil War cavalry encampment.

Colonel: I have the honor to report the arrival of my advance at this place on yesterday morning at 11 o'clock, and deem it proper to give the lieutenant-general commanding a report of the condition of the country through which I have passed, also the state of affairs as they exist, with such suggestions as would naturally arise from observations made and a personal knowledge of facts as they exist. From Tupelo to Purdy the country has been laid waste, and unless some effort is made either by the Mobile and Ohio Railroad Company or the Government[,] the people are bound to suffer for food. They have been[,] by the enemy and by roving bands of deserters and tories[,] stripped of everything; have neither negroes nor stock with which to raise a crop or make a support. What provisions they had have been consumed or taken from them, and the majority of families are bound to suffer. They are now hauling corn in ox wagons and by hand-cars from Okolona and below to Corinth, and as far north as Purdy, also east and west of Corinth, on the Memphis and Charleston Railroad, but their limited means of transportation will not enable them to subsist their families, and my opinion is that the railroad can be easily and speedily repaired, and that any deficiency in iron from Meridian north can be supplied from the Memphis and Charleston Railroad, and that a brigade of cavalry with a regiment or two of infantry placed at Corinth would afford protection to that section, and would be the means of driving out of the country or placing in our army the deserters and tories infesting that region, whose lawless appropriation of provisions, horses, and other property is starving out the defenseless and unprotected citizens of a large scope of country. Repairing and running the railroad would enable the inhabitants to procure provisions from the prairies and would prove an invaluable acquisition in the transportation of supplies and troops from this section. But little can be done in returning the deserters from our army now in West Tennessee, and collecting and sending out all persons subject to military duty, unless the railroad is rebuilt or repaired, as they will have to be marched through a country already, for want of labor and supplies, insufficient for the subsistence of its own inhabitants. With a conscript post or an established military post at Corinth and the railroad from thence south they could be rapidly forwarded to the army. The wires can also be extended and a telegraph office established. The whole of West Tennessee is overrun by bands and squads of robbers, horse thieves, and deserters, whose depredations and unlawful appropriations of private property are rapidly and effectually depleting the country. The Federal forces at Paducah, Columbus, and Union City are small. There is also a small force at Fort Heiman, on the Tennessee, and Fort Pillow, on the Mississippi River. About 2,000 men of Smith's forces, composed of parts of many regiments, have crossed the Tennessee River at Clifton and Fort Heiman, and returned to Nashville; four regiments of Illinois cavalry have re-enlisted and have gone home on furlough. The cavalry force at Memphis is therefore small.

"Numerous reports having reached me of the wanton destruction of property by Col. Fielding Hurst and his regiment of renegade Tennesseans, I ordered Lieut. Col. W. M. Reed to investigate and report upon the same, and herewith transmit you a copy of his report. Have thought it both just and proper to bring these transactions to the notice of the Federal commander at Memphis, and by flag of truce will demand of him the restitution of the money taken from the citizens of Jackson, under a threat from Hurst to burn the town unless the money was forthcoming at an appointed time. Have also demanded that the murderers be delivered up to Confederate authority for punishment, and reply from that officer as to the demand, &c., will be forwarded you as soon as received. Should the Federal commander refuse to accede to the just demands made, I have instructed the officer in charge of the flag to deliver the notice inclosed outlawing Hurst and his command. I am, general, very respectfully, your obedient servant, N. B. Forrest, Major-General."[97]

*Still angry over the outrages of Union General Hurst, Forrest fired off this dispatch on March 22, 1864:*
☞ "In the Field, March 22, 1864. To whom it may concern: Whereas it has come to the knowledge of the major-general commanding that Col. Fielding Hurst, commanding [Sixth] Regiment U.S. [Tennessee Cavalry] Volunteers, has been guilty of wanton extortion upon the citizens of Jackson, Tenn., and other places, guilty of depredations upon private property, guilty of house burning, guilty of murders, both of citizens and soldiers of the Confederate States; and whereas demand has been duly made upon the military authorities of the United States for the surrender of said Col. Fielding Hurst and such officers and men of his command as are guilty of these outrages; and whereas this just demand has been refused by said authorities: I therefore declare the aforesaid Fielding Hurst, and the officers and men of his command, outlaws, and not entitled to be treated as prisoners of war falling into the hands of the forces of the Confederate States. N. B. Forrest, Major- General, Commanding."[98]

*On April 12, 1864, Forrest fought at the infamous Battle of Fort Pillow, where, according to Yankee mythology, the General and his men slaughtered surrendering Union soldiers, disproportionately targeting black Union soldiers. I have discussed this slanderous anti-South propaganda at length in my work* A Rebel Born *and so need not go over the same territory here. Instead, I will provide examples of Forrest's reports concerning the engagement. The first is a battlefield dispatch from Forrest to Union Major Lionel F. Booth, commander of Yankee forces at the conflict:*
☞ "Headquarters Confederate Cavalry, near Fort Pillow, April 12, 1864. Major Booth, Commanding U. S. Forces, Fort Pillow: Major: The conduct of the officers and men garrisoning Fort Pillow has been such as to entitle them to being treated as prisoners of war. I demand the unconditional surrender of the entire garrison, promising that you

Cavalry horses were often kept in enormous stables, like this one photographed in Arlington, Virginia, in the Summer of 1861.

shall be treated as prisoners of war. My men have just received a fresh supply of ammunition, and from their present position can easily assault and capture the fort. Should my demand be refused, I cannot be responsible for the fate of your command. Respectfully, N. B. Forrest, Major-General, Commanding."[99]

*Forrest sent this report concerning the Battle of Fort Pillow to his superior General Leonidas Polk on April 15, 1864:*
☞ "Jackson, Tenn., April 15, 1864. General: I attacked Fort Pillow on the morning of the 12$^{th}$ instant with a part of Bell's and McCulloch's brigades, numbering 1,500, under Brig. Gen. James R. Chalmers. After a short fight drove the enemy, 700 strong, into the fort under the cover of their gun-boats. Demanded a surrender, which was declined by Maj. L. F. Booth commanding U. S. forces. I stormed the fort, and after a contest of thirty minutes captured the entire garrison, killing 500 and taking 200 horses and a large amount of quartermaster's stores. The officers in the fort were killed, including Major Booth. I sustained a loss of 20 killed and 60 wounded. Among the wounded is the gallant Lieut. Col. Wiley M. Reed while leading the Fifth Mississippi. Over 100 citizens who had fled to the fort to escape conscription ran into the river and were drowned. The Confederate flag now floats over the fort. N. B. Forrest, Major-General."[100]

# THE QUOTABLE NATHAN BEDFORD FORREST  71

*What follows is General Forrest's full official field report of the Battle of Fort Pillow. Written on April 26, 1864, it completely contradicts the fictitious Northern version of events:*

☞ "Headquarters Forrest's Cavalry Department, Jackson, Tenn., April 26, 1864. Colonel: I have the honor respectfully to forward you the following report of my engagement with the enemy on the 12$^{th}$ instant at Fort Pillow:

In February 1862, when his superiors rashly decided to surrender Fort Donelson to Union General Ulysses S. Grant, Forrest stubbornly refused to go along. Instead, he secretly and efficiently evacuated his troops, sparing hundreds of Confederate soldiers imprisonment, torture, and even death at the hands of the Yankee invaders. While pro-North supporters call the act "cowardly," we in the South call it "ingenious"!

"My command consisted of McCulloch's brigade, of Chalmers' division, and Bell's brigade, of Buford's division, both placed for the expedition under the command of Brig. Gen. James R. Chalmers, who, by a forced march, drove in the enemy's pickets, gained possession of the outer works, and by the time I reached the field, at 10 a.m., had forced the enemy to their main fortifications, situated on the bluff or bank of the Mississippi River at the mouth of Cold Creek. The fort is an earth-work, crescent shaped, is 8 feet in height and 4 feet across the top, surrounded by a ditch 6 feet deep and 12 feet in width, walls sloping to the ditch but perpendicular inside. It was garrisoned by 700 troops with six pieces of field artillery. A deep ravine surrounds the fort, and from the fort to the ravine the ground descends rapidly. Assuming command, I ordered General Chalmers to advance his lines and gain position on the slope, where our men would be perfectly protected from the heavy fire of artillery and musketry, as the enemy could not depress their pieces so as to rake the slopes, nor could they fire on them with small-arms except by mounting the breast-works and exposing themselves to the fire of our sharpshooters, who, under cover of stumps and logs, forced them to keep down inside the works. After several hours hard fighting the desired position was gained, not, however, without considerable loss. Our main line was now within an average distance of 100 yards from the fort, and extended from Cold Creek, on the right, to the bluff, or bank, of the Mississippi River on the left.

"During the entire morning the gun-boat kept up a continued fire in all directions, but without effect, and being confident of my ability to take the fort by assault, and desiring to prevent further loss of life, I sent, under flag of truce, a demand for the unconditional surrender of the garrison, a copy of which demand is hereto appended, marked No. 1, to which I received a reply, marked No. 2. The gun-boat had ceased firing, but the smoke of three other boats ascending the river was in view, the foremost boat apparently crowded with troops, and believing the request for an hour was to gain time for re-enforcements to arrive, and that the desire to consult the officers of the gun-boat was a pretext by which they desired improperly to communicate with her, I at once sent this reply, copy of which is numbered 3, directing Captain [W. A.] Goodman, assistant adjutant-general of Brigadier-General Chalmers, who bore the flag, to remain until he received a reply or until the expiration of the time proposed.

"My dispositions had all been made, and my forces were in a position that would enable me to take the fort with less loss than to have withdrawn under fire, and it seemed to me so perfectly apparent to the garrison that such was the case, that I deemed their [capture] without further bloodshed a certainty. After some little delay, seeing a message delivered to Captain Goodman, I rode up myself to where the notes were received and delivered. The answer was handed me, written in pencil on a slip of paper, without envelope, and was, as well as I remember, in these words: "Negotiations will not attain the desired object." As the officers who were in charge of the Federal flag of truce had expressed a doubt as to my presence, and had pronounced the demand a trick, I handed them back the note saying: "I am General Forrest; go back and say to Major Booth that I demand an answer in plain, unmistakable English. Will he fight or surrender?" Returning to my original position, before the expiration of twenty minutes I received a reply, copy of which is marked No. 4.

"While these negotiations were pending the steamers from below were rapidly approaching the fort. The foremost was the *Olive Branch*, whose position and movements indicated her intention to land. A few shots fired into her caused her to leave the shore and make for the opposite. One other boat passed up on the far side of the river, the third one turned back.

Colonel William A. Johnson commanded a brigade in Forrest's Cavalry.

"The time having expired, I directed Brigadier-General Chalmers to prepare for the assault. Bell's brigade occupied the right, with his extreme right resting on Coal Creek. McCulloch's brigade occupied the left, extending from the center to the river. Three companies of his left regiment were placed in an old rifle-pit on the left and almost in the rear of the fort, which had evidently been thrown up for the protection of sharpshooters or riflemen in supporting the water batteries below. On the right a portion of Barteau's regiment, of Bell's brigade, was also under the bluff and in rear of the fort. I dispatched staff officers to Colonels Bell and McCulloch, commanding brigades, to say to them that I should watch with interest the conduct of the troops; that Missourians, Mississippians, and Tennesseans surrounded the works, and I desired to see who would first scale the fort. Fearing the gun-boats and transports might attempt a landing, I directed my aide-de-camp, Capt. Charles W. Anderson, to assume command of the three companies on the left and rear of the fort and hold the position against anything that might come by land or water, but to take no part in the assault on the fort. Everything being ready, the bugle sounded the charge, which was made with a yell, and the works carried without a perceptible halt in any part of the line. As our troops mounted and poured into the fortification the enemy retreated toward the river, arms in hand and firing back, and their colors flying, no doubt expecting the gun-boat to shell us away from the bluff and protect them until they could be taken off or re-enforced. As they descended the bank an enfilading and deadly fire was poured into them by the troops under Captain Anderson, on the left, and Barteau's detachment on the right. Until this fire was opened upon them, at a distance varying from 30 to 100 yards, they were evidently ignorant of any force having gained their rear. The regiments which had stormed and carried the fort also poured a destructive fire into the rear of the retreating and now panic-stricken and almost decimated garrison. Fortunately for those of the enemy who survived this short but desperate struggle, some of our men cut the halyards, and the United States flag, floating from a tall mast in the center of the fort, came down. The forces stationed in the rear of the fort could see the flag, but were too far under the bluff to see the fort, and when the flag descended they ceased firing. But for this, so near were they to the enemy that few, if any, would have survived unhurt another volley. As it was, many rushed into the river and were drowned, and the actual loss of life will perhaps never be known, as there were quite a number of refugee citizens in the fort, many of whom were drowned and several killed in the retreat from the fort. In less than twenty minutes from the time the bugles sounded the charge, firing had ceased, and the work was done. One of the Parrott guns was turned on the gun-boat. She steamed off without replying. She had, as I afterward understood, expended all her ammunition, and was therefore powerless in affording the Federal garrison the aid and protection they doubtless expected of her when they retreated toward the river. Details were made, consisting of the captured Federals and negroes, in charge of their own officers, to collect together and bury the dead, which work continued until dark.

"I also directed Captain Anderson to procure a skiff and take with him Captain Young, a captured Federal officer, and deliver to Captain Marshall, of the gun-boat, the message, copy of which is appended and numbered 5. All the boats and skiffs having been taken off by citizens escaping from the fort during the engagement, the message could not be delivered, although every effort was made to induce Captain Marshall to send his boat ashore by raising a white flag, with which Captain Young walked up and down the river in vain signaling her to come in or send out a boat. She finally moved off and disappeared around the bend above the fort. General Chalmers withdrew his forces from the fort before dark and encamped a few miles east of it.

The "fightin' preacher," officer David C. Kelley, was a well respected brigade commander in Forrest's Cavalry. On the battlefield Forrest sometimes made use of Kelley's special relationship with God.

"On the morning of the 13th, I again dispatched Captain Anderson to Fort Pillow for the purpose of placing, if possible, the Federal wounded on board their transports, and report to me on his return the condition of affairs at the river. I respectfully refer you to his report, numbered 6.

"My loss in the engagement was 20 killed and 60 wounded. That of the enemy unknown. Two hundred and twenty-eight were buried on the evening of the battle, and quite a number were buried the next day by details from the gun-boat fleet.

"We captured 6 pieces of artillery, viz., two 10-pounder Parrott guns, two 12-pounder howitzers, and two brass 6-pounder guns, and about 350 stand of small-arms. The balance of the small-arms had been thrown in the river. All the small-arms were picked up where the enemy fell or threw them down. A few were in the fort, the balance scattered from the top of the hill to the water's edge.

"We captured 164 Federals, 75 negro troops, and about 40 negro women and children, and after removing everything of value as far as able to do so, the warehouses, tents, &c., were destroyed by fire.

"Among our severely wounded is Lieut. Col. Wiley M. Reed, assigned temporarily to the command of the Fifth Mississippi Regiment, who fell severely wounded while leading his regiment. When carried from the field he was supposed to be mortally wounded, but hopes are entertained of his ultimate recovery. He is a brave and gallant officer, a courteous gentleman, and a consistent Christian minister.

"I cannot compliment too highly the conduct of Colonels Bell and McCulloch and the officers and men of their brigades, which composed the forces of Brigadier-General Chalmers. They fought with courage and intrepidity, and, without bayonets, assaulted and carried one of the strongest fortifications in the country.

"On the 15th, at Brownsville, I received orders which rendered it necessary to send General Chalmers, in command of his own division and Bell's brigade, southward; hence I have no official report from him, but will, as soon as it can be obtained, forward a complete list of our killed and wounded, which has been ordered made out and forwarded at the earliest possible moment.

"In closing my report I desire to acknowledge the prompt and energetic action of Brigadier-General Chalmers, commanding the forces around Fort Pillow. His faithful execution of all movements necessary to the successful accomplishment of the object of the expedition entitles him to special mention. He has reason to be proud of the conduct of the officers and men of his command for their gallantry and courage in assaulting and carrying the enemy's work without the assistance of artillery or bayonets.

"To my staff, as heretofore, my acknowledgments are due for their prompt and faithful delivery of all orders. I am, colonel, very respectfully, your obedient servant, N. B. Forrest, Major-General, Commanding."[101]

*At the Battle of Brice's Cross Roads (also known as the Battle of Tishomingo*

This photo shows a Yankee cavalry unit guarding a Union wagon train traveling along the Rappahannock River in Virginia in the Autumn of 1862. Forrest's "critter company," as his cavalry was affectionately known, would have looked very similar.

Creek) on June 10, 1864, Forrest led his men in one of the most decisive and brilliant Confederate victories of the entire War. A few weeks later the General gave these moving words to his men:

☞ "Headquarters Forrest's Cavalry, Tupelo, Miss., June 28, 1864. Soldiers: After a long and laborious campaign, the major-general commanding deems it an appropriate occasion to address you a few words of recapitulation, acknowledgment, and congratulation. About the 15th of February last the campaign which so gloriously terminated at Tishomingo Creek was inaugurated. Major-General Sherman with a large and well-appointed army undertook to penetrate the central counties of Alabama and Mississippi. His object was avowedly to capture Selma and Mobile, and to desolate that productive region of country, from which the granaries of a large section of the Confederacy were supplied. Generals Smith and Grierson had their duties assigned them, and were to act a conspicuous part in the work of spoliation and piracy. With a large co-operating cavalry force, thoroughly armed and equipped, they were to descend through Northern Mississippi, carrying fire and sword with them. On they came, like a blighting sirocco [storm]. At West Point you met them. There you threw yourselves across the rich prairies, a living bulwark, to stay the desolating tide. Compared with the enemy you were but few in numbers, but every man became a hero, for all seemed impressed with the importance of the momentous struggle. You proved yourselves equal to the expectations of the country. You met the proud and exultant enemy. The result is known to the world; you drove him howling back in ignominy and shame; broken and demoralized. Sherman's campaign was thus brought to an abrupt conclusion, and Mississippi and Alabama saved. The victory was a glorious one, and with heartfelt pride the general commanding acknowledges your unexampled gallantry. This great work was accomplished by Colonel Bell's brigade, commanded by Colonel Barteau, Colonel McCulloch's, and Colonel Forrest's brigades. But great as was this victory, it is not without its alloy. The laurel is closely entwined with the cypress, and the luster of a brilliant triumph is darkened by the blood with which it was purchased. It was here that Colonel [James A.] Barksdale gave up his life[,] a willing sacrifice upon the altar of his country. He fell in front of the battle, gallantly discharging his duty. He sleeps, but his name is imperishable. Here, too, fell the noble brother of the general commanding, Col. Jeffrey E. Forrest. He was a brave and chivalrous spirit, ever foremost in the fight. He fell in the flower of his youth and usefulness, but his dying gaze was proudly turned upon the victorious field, which his own valor had aided in winning. Peace to the ashes of these gallant young heroes.

"After a short repose you were called to a new theater of action. By long and rapid marches, which you endured without murmur or complaint, you found yourselves upon the waters of the Ohio, sweeping the enemy before you wherever you met him, capturing hundreds of prisoners, valuable and needed stores in the quartermaster's and ordnance departments, while securing for yourselves a character for endurance, valor, and efficiency which might well excite the envy of the most famous legions in military history. At Fort Pillow you exhibited the same conspicuous gallantry. In the face of a murderous fire from two gun-boats and six pieces of artillery on the fort, you stormed the works and either killed or captured the entire garrison, a motley herd of negroes, traitors, and Yankees. This noble work was accomplished by parts of Chalmers' and Buford's divisions, composed of Bell's and McCulloch's brigades, commanded by Brigadier-General Chalmers; and for his gallantry on this and other occasions General Chalmers deserves the enduring gratitude of his countrymen. For the exhibitions of high soldierly bearing on these fields you have earned from your country and its government the most grateful and well-deserved plaudits. Congress has voted you complimentary resolutions of thanks and tendered you a nation's homage.

"But the crowning glory of your great deeds has yet to be named. Tishomingo Creek is the brightest leaf in your chaplets of laurels. General Grierson, not satisfied with his test of your prowess,

Except for the letters "U.S." on the saddle, this Yankee cavalry officer's mount was nearly identical to the Confederate cavalry officer's mount.

united with General Sturgis, at the head of one of the best appointed forces ever equipped by the Yankee nation, complete in infantry, cavalry, artillery, and supply trains. They came forth with threats of vengeance toward you and your commander for the bloody victory of Fort Pillow, made a massacre only by dastardly Yankee reporters. Again you responded bravely to your general's call. You met the enemy and defeated him. Victory was never more glorious, disaster never more crushing and signal. From a proud and defiant foe, en route to the heart of your country, with declarations both by negro and white troops of "no quarters to Forrest or his men," he became an enemy beaten, defeated, routed, destroyed. You drove the boasted minions of despotism in confused flight from the battle-field. Seventeen guns, 250 wagons, 3,000 stand of arms, 2,000 prisoners, and killed and wounded 2,000 more, are the proud trophies which adorn your triumphant banners. The remainder is still wandering in the bushes and bottoms, forever lost to the enemy. There were not over 3,000 of you who achieved this victory over 10,000 of the enemy. Had you never before raised an arm in your country's cause this terrible overthrow of her brutal foe would entitle you to her deepest gratitude. Again, your general expresses his pride and admiration of your gallantry and wonderful achievements. You stand before the world an unconquerable band of heroes. Whether dismounted, and fighting shoulder to shoulder like infantry veterans, or hurling your irresistible squadrons on the flying foe, you evinced the same courageous bravery.

"Soldiers! Amid your rejoicing do not forget the gallant dead upon these fields of glory. Many a noble comrade has fallen[,] a costly sacrifice to his country's independence. The most you can do is to cherish their memory and strive to make the future as glorious as you and they have made the past.

"To Brigadier-General Buford, commanding division, my obligations are especially due. His gallantry and activity on the field were ever conspicuous, and for the energy displayed in pursuing the enemy he deserves much of his Government. He has abundant cause to be proud of his brigade commanders, Colonels Lyon and Bell, who displayed great gallantry during the day. Col. Edward Winchester Rucker was prompt in the discharge of every duty. His brigade displayed conspicuous steadiness during the fight. Colonel Johnson, commanding brigade from General Roddey's command, merits notice for his coolness and bravery on this occasion, and for the valuable services rendered by his troops. Nor can the general commanding forget to mention the efficient aid rendered by the artillery, commanded by Capt. John W. Morton. He moved rapidly over the roughest ground and was always in action at the right time, and his well-directed fire dealt destruction in the masses of the enemy. The general commanding also takes pleasure in noticing the intelligent alacrity with which Maj. C. W. Anderson, Capt. W. H. Brand, Lieutenants Otey, Donelson, Titus, and Galloway, of my staff, conveyed orders to all parts of the field. They were ever near my person, and were prompt in the discharge of every duty.

"Soldiers! You have done much, but there is still work for you to do. By prompt obedience to orders and patient endurance you will be enabled to repeat these great achievements. The enemy is again preparing to break through the living wall erected by your noble bosoms and big hearts. In the name and recollection of ruined home, desolated fields and the bleaching bones of your martyred comrades, you are appealed to again. The smoke of your burning homesteads, the screams of your insulted women, and the cries of starving children will again nerve your strong arms with strength. Your fathers of '76 had much to fight for, but how little and unimportant was their cause compared with yours. They fought not against annihilation, but simply to be independent of a foreign yet a constitutional and free Government. You are struggling against the most odious of all tyranny, for existence itself, for your property, your homes, your wives, and children, against your own enslavement, against emancipation, confiscation, and subjugation, with all their attendant horrors.

"In conclusion, your commanding general congratulates you on the brilliant prospects which everywhere pervade our cause. The independence of the Confederate States is a fixed, accomplished, immutable fact. The ray of peace is glimmering like bright sunshine around the dark clouds. Be true to yourselves and your country a little while longer and you will soon be enabled to return to your desolated homes, there to collect together once more your scattered household goods."[102]

*What follows is a typical Forrest dispatch, demanding the enemy's immediate surrender. This one was issued on September 24, 1864:*

☛ "Headquarters Forrest's Cavalry, in the Field, September 24, 1864. Officer Commanding U. S. Forces, Athens, Alabama: I demand an immediate and unconditional surrender of the entire force and all government stores and property at this post. I have a sufficient force to storm and take your works, and if I am forced to do so the responsibility of the consequences must rest with you. Should you, however, accept the terms, all white soldiers shall be treated as prisoners of war and the negroes returned to their masters. A reply is requested immediately. Respectfully, N. B. Forrest, Major-General C. 5. Army."[103]

Brigadier General William Hicks "Red" Jackson commanded a division of Forrest's Cavalry. Jackson married a close cousin of the author (who descends from the Hardings of Virginia and Tennessee): Selene Harding, daughter of General William Giles Harding of Belle Meade Plantation (Nashville, Tennessee) and Elizabeth Irwin McGavock of Carnton Plantation (Franklin, Tennessee).

*On October 8, 1864, from Cherokee, Alabama, a by now exhausted Forrest sent the following request to his superior General Richard Taylor (son of U.S. President Zachary Taylor and President Davis' former brother-in-law):*

☛ "Headquarters Forrest's Cavalry, Cherokee, October 8, 1864. Lieut. Gen. R. Taylor, General: I have been constantly in the field since 1861, and have spent half the entire time in the saddle. I have never asked for a furlough for over ten days in which to rest and recruit, and except when wounded and unable to leave my bed have had no respite from duty. My strength is failing and it is absolutely necessary that I should have some rest. I left a large estate [Green Grove, at Sunflower Landing] in Mississippi and have never given my private affairs a day's attention at any one time since the war began. . . . I respectfully ask that my two divisions be placed as they originally were under the command of

Brigadier-Generals Chalmers and Buford, and that Mabry's brigade be substituted for McCulloch's, which change would in my opinion be satisfactory to all parties. I have captured since I came into this department over 30 pieces of artillery, fitting up my command with four batteries (in all sixteen guns). They are now scattered, and I desire if possible to get all my command together, and with General Chalmers as senior officer feel that it would be safe to leave the command for a short time, which in my present state of health is absolutely necessary and which you will confer a favor on me by granting as early as consistent with the good of the service. I am, general, very respectfully, your obedient servant, N. B. Forrest, Major-General."[104]

*On October 17, 1864, Forrest issued his report on his recent "Operations in Northern Alabama and Middle Tennessee." In it he commented on the heroic behavior of some of his men:*

☞ "I take pleasure . . . in calling the notice of the [Confederate] Government to the conduct of Colonel [David C.] Kelley, commanding Colonel [Edmund W.] Rucker's brigade. He displayed all the dash, energy, and gallantry which has so long made him an efficient officer, and justly merits promotion by his Government. The conduct of Lieut. Col. Jesse A. Forrest [one of the General's younger brothers] at Athens, Ala., is worthy of mention. While the enemy was attempting to re-enforce the fort, at the head of his splendid regiment, Colonel Forrest made a gallant charge, driving the enemy from his position, but in this charge he received a severe wound in the thigh. The splendid discipline of Col. James M. Warren's troops, of General Roddey's command, attracted my attention and received my commendation on the field. They moved forward in perfect order and with the steadiness of veteran soldiers. Colonel Warren has few superiors in the service, and is entitled to special mention for his uniform gallantry."[105]

*On November 12, 1864, having by then heard about the reelection of the treasonous, and treacherous, liberal Lincoln to a second term (on November 8), Forrest took a few moments to send a thank-you note to General Richard Taylor, one of the few Confederate officers the Tennessean actually respected. The missive reveals both the deeply personal relationship the two had forged and Forrest's undying devotion to the Confederate Cause:*

☞ "Headquarters Forrest's Cavalry, Corinth, November 12, 1864. Lieut. Gen. R. Taylor: General: In a few days I will forward you a report of my recent operations on the Tennessee River, together with a report of my expedition to Memphis. These two documents will, I presume, for the present terminate my official connection with you, an event which I deeply deplore. Our intercourse has not been of long duration, but to me it has been most pleasant and agreeable, certainly of such a character as to render our separation a source of regret, but duty calls me elsewhere. I go to share in the toils and, I trust, in the victories of other fields, but in leaving you I shall carry with me a sincere friendship made so by your kindness and official courtesy. I congratulate you on leaving that so much of the territory under your jurisdiction has been rescued from the grasp of the invader. Twelve months ago I entered your department and found the people groaning under the most cruel and merciless oppression. They were despondent and traitors exultant. I leave the department in security and the people hopeful. The unprincipled, uncivilized, and destroying foe has been driven to other fields where the strong arms of patriots are still striving to chastise his atrocities. I know not how long we are to labor for that independence for which we have thus far struggled in vain, but this I do know that I will never weary in defending our cause, which must ultimately triumph. Faith is the duty of the hour. We will succeed. We have only to 'work and wait.' Be assured, my dear general, that wherever I may go, I shall deeply sympathize in all that concerns your interest and always exult in your success. With great respect, I am, general, your friend and obedient servant, N. B. Forrest, Major-General."[106]

Brigadier General James R. Chalmers commanded a division of Forrest's Cavalry, performing most notably in General John Bell Hood's West Tennessee Campaign of 1864. Though the two did not always get along, Forrest praised Chalmers for his courage and talents on the battlefield.

*By this time in the War Forrest was well adept, and well-known, for striking fear and confusion in the hearts of Yankees. A favorite pastime of his was to overrun undermanned garrisons and outposts. He was also particularly good at wreaking devastation on the Union supply lines, not only in his home-state, but all across the South. Throughout Tennessee, for example, he broke apart and tore up railroad tracks, bombed train stations, burned Yankee blockhouses, stockades, and sawmills, dynamited bridges and trestles, destroyed culverts and viaducts, cut telegraph wires, disabled field artillery, fired warehouses, sank supply ships, transport ships, and gunboats, and easily captured Yankee supply trains, depots, and garrisons.*[107] *One of his favorite methods of ruining railroads was to build fires along their length. It required little effort on the part of his men and caused the metal tracks to expand, crack, and buckle, rendering them unusable.*[108] *And unlike Yankee wrecking crews (who seldom did more than superficial damage to railroads), the destruction heaped upon rail lines by Forrest's men left them completely demolished and irreparable.*[109] *In making life wretched for the enemy at every turn, he dispirited the Yanks, bought precious time, and bolstered Southern pride. What galled Northerners most was Forrest's capture and destruction, in Tennessee, of $6.7 million (the equivalent of about $91 million today) worth of Yankee machinery, along with a gunboat fleet at Johnsonville. In his official report of the raid, known as the Battle of Johnsonville (November 4-5, 1864), Forrest wrote with barely concealed relish:*

☞ "Headquarters Forrest's Cavalry Corps, Verona, Miss., January 12, 1865. Colonel: Continued active service in the field for two months has prevented me from reporting at an earlier day the action of my troops on the expedition along the Tennessee River. I avail myself; however, of the first leisure moment, and have the honor of submitting the following report:

"On the 16th of October I ordered Colonel [Tyree H.] Bell to move with his brigade from Corinth and to form a camp at Lavinia. On the 18th Brigadier-General [Abe] Buford was ordered to move with the Kentucky brigade to Lexington for the purpose of watching General [Edward] Hatch, who was reported to be in that direction. I moved from Corinth on the morning of the 19th, with my escort and [Edmund W.] Rucker's brigade, to Jackson, Tenn. At this place I was joined by Brigadier-General [James R.] Chalmers with about 250 men of McCulloch's brigade and 300 of Mabry's brigade, which, with Rucker's brigade, constituted his division. On the 29th I ordered him to proceed

Second Lieutenant George Limerick Cowan of Forrest's Escort. Cowan was related to Forrest's wife, Mary Ann Montgomery, whose mother was Elizabeth Cowan of Blount County, Tennessee. George married the author's cousin, Hattie McGavock, whose father Randal McGavock built famous Carnton Plantation in Franklin, Williamson County, Tennessee.

to the Tennessee River and there co-operate with Brigadier-General Buford, who was blockading the river at Fort Heiman and Paris Landing. On arriving at the river I found it most effectually blockaded by a judicious disposition of the troops and batteries sent for this purpose.

"On the morning of the 29th the steamer *Mazeppa*, with two barges in tow, made her appearance. As she passed the battery at Fort Heiman, supported by Brigadier-General Lyon, she was fired upon by one section of Morton's battery and two 20-pounder Parrott guns. Every shot must have taken effect, as she made for the shore after the third fire and reached the opposite bank in a disabled condition, where she was abandoned by the crew and passengers, who fled to the woods. A hawser was erected on this side of the river and she was towed over, and on being boarded she was found to be heavily loaded with blankets, shoes, clothing, hard bread, &c. While her cargo was being removed to the shore three gun-boats made their appearance, and commenced shelling the men who were engaged in unloading the *Mazeppa*. They were forced to retire, and fearing the boat might be captured Brigadier-General Buford ordered her to be burned.

"On the 30th the steamer *Anna* came down the river and succeeded in passing both the upper and lower batteries, but was so disabled that she sunk before she reached Paducah. The *Anna* was followed by two transports (*J. W. Cheeseman*, the *Venus*) and two barges under convoy of gun-boat *Undine*. In attempting to pass my batteries all the boats were disabled. They landed on the opposite side of the river and were abandoned by the crews, who left their dead and wounded.

Lieutenant-Colonel Kelley, with two companies of his regiment, was thrown across the river and soon returned to Paris Landing with the boats. The steamer *J. W. Cheeseman* was so disabled that she was ordered, with the two barges, to be burned; the gun-boat was also burned while moving up the river to Johnsonville. The *Venus* was recaptured by the enemy on (November 2,) but was destroyed the next day (November 4) at Johnsonville by my batteries.

"On the 1$^{st}$ of November I ordered my command to move in the direction of Johnsonville, which place I reached on the 3d. At this point Colonel Mabry joined General Chalmers with [James C.] Thrall's battery. The wharf at Johnsonville was lined with transports and gun-boats. An immense warehouse presented itself and was represented as being stored with the most valuable supplies, while several acres of the shore were covered with every description of army stores. The fort was situated on a high hill and in a commanding position, and defended by strong works.

"All my troops having arrived, I commenced disposing of them with a view of bombarding the enemy. As he commanded the position I designed to occupy, I was necessarily compelled to act with great caution. I planted most of my guns during the night, and while completing the work the next morning my men worked behind ambuscades, which obscured everything from the enemy. Thrall's battery of howitzers was placed in position above Johnsonville, while Morton's and Hudson's batteries were placed nearly opposite and just below town.

"I ordered a simultaneous assault to commence at 3 o'clock. All my movements for twenty-four hours had been so secretive the enemy seemed to think I had retired, and for the purpose of making a reconnaissance two gun-boats were lashed together and pushed out just before the attack opened. The bombardment commenced by the section of Morton's battery commanded by Lieutenant Brown. The other batteries joined promptly in the assault. The enemy returned the fire from twenty-eight guns on their gun-boats and fourteen guns on the hill. About fifty guns were thus engaged at the same time, and the firing was terrific. The gun-boats, in fifteen minutes after the engagement commenced, were set on fire, and made rapidly for the shore, where they were both consumed. My batteries next opened upon the transports, and in a short time they were in flames. The immense amount of stores were also set on fire, together with the huge warehouse above time landing. By night the wharf for nearly one mile up and down the river presented one solid sheet of flame. The enemy continued a furious cannonading on my batteries.

"Having completed the work designed by the expedition, I moved my command six miles during the night by the light of the enemy's burning property. The roads were almost impassable, and the march to Corinth was slow and toilsome, but I reached there on November 10, after an absence of over two weeks, during which time I captured and destroyed 4 gun-boats, 14 transports, 20 barges, 26 pieces of artillery, $6,700,000 worth of property, and 150 prisoners. Brigadier-General Buford, after supplying his own command, turned over to my chief quartermaster about 9,000 pairs of shoes and 1,000 blankets.

"My loss during the entire trip was 2 killed and 9 wounded; that of the enemy will probably reach 500 killed, wounded, and prisoners.

Brigadier General Frank C. Armstrong commanded a division of Forrest's cavalry and was highly valued by the General.

"On this expedition my division commanders, Brigadier-Generals Chalmers and Buford, displayed the same prompt observance in obeying orders, the same skill, coolness, and undaunted courage which they have heretofore exhibited, and for which I thank them.

"My brigade commanders, Colonels Bell, Rucker, Crossland, and Mabry, are deserving of the highest commendation for their conduct on this as on all former occasions.

"Brigadier-General Lyon, who had been assigned to another

department, reported to me on this expedition and rendered much valuable service at Johnsonville and Fort Heiman.

"To Capt. John W. Morton, acting chief of artillery, and the brave troops under his command, my thanks are especially due for their efficiency and gallantry on this expedition. They fired with a rapidity and accuracy which extorted the commendation of even the enemy. The rammers were shot from the hands of the cannoneers, some of whom were nearly buried amid the dirt which was thrown upon them by the storm of shell which rained upon them by the enemy's batteries. All of which is respectfully submitted. N. B. Forrest, Major-General.[110]

*In early 1865 General Forrest predicted the outcome of Lincoln's War:*
☞ "To my mind it is evident that the end is not far off; it will only be a question of time as to when General Lee's lines at Petersburg will be broken, for Grant is wearing him out; with unlimited resources of men and money, he must ultimately force Lee to leave Virginia or surrender. Lee's army will never leave Virginia; they will not follow him out when the time comes, and that will end the war."[111]

*Though, on April 9, 1865, Lincoln's War had finally come to an end, Forrest, a natural-born warrior who loved the manly, open-air life of the soldier, could not bear to put his weapons down. There was something in him that could simply not accept defeat or offer capitulation, and for a few days, in vain hope, he considered the story of Lee's surrender nothing more than Yankee disinformation, as his April 25th-general order to his men indicates:*
☞ "Headquarters Forrest's Cavalry Corps, in the field, April 25, 1865. Soldiers: the enemy have originated and sent through our lines various and conflicting dispatches indicating the surrender of General Robert E. Lee and the Army of Northern Virginia. A morbid appetite for news and sensation rumors has magnified a simple flag of truce from Lieutenant General Taylor to General Canby at Mobile into a mission for negotiating the terms of surrender of the troops of his department. Your commanding general desires to say to you that no credence should be given to such reports; nor should they for a moment control the actions or influence the feelings, sentiments, or conduct of the troops of this command. On the contrary, from Southern sources and now published in our papers, it is reported that General Lee has not surrendered; that

An orderly caring for an officer's mount.

a cessation of hostilities has been agreed upon between Generals Johnston and Sherman for the purpose of adjusting the difficulties and differences now existing between the Confederate and the United States of America. Also that since the evacuation of Richmond and the death of Abraham Lincoln, Grant has lost in battle and by desertion 100,000 men. As your commander he further assures you that at this time, above all others, it is the duty of every man to stand firm at his post and true to his colors. Your past services, your gallant and heroic conduct on many victorious fields, forbid the thought that you will ever ground your arms except with honor. Duty to your country, to yourselves, and the gallant dead who have fallen in this great struggle for liberty and independence, demand that every man should continue to do his whole duty. With undiminished confidence in your courage and fortitude, and knowing you now will not disregard the claims of honor, patriotism, and manhood, and those of the women and children of the country, so long defended by your strong arms and willing hearts, he announces his determination to stand by you, stay with you, and lead you to the end. A few days more will determine the truth or falsity of all the reports now in circulation. In the meantime let those who are now absent from their commands for the purpose of mounting themselves, or otherwise, return without delay. In conclusion, be firm and unwavering, discharging promptly and faithfully every duty devolving upon you. Preserve untarnished the reputation you have so nobly won, and leave results to Him who in wisdom controls and governs all things. N. B. Forrest, Lieutenant- General."[112]

*In Gainesville, Alabama, on May 9, 1865, the General bid farewell to his soldiers as only a man like Forrest could. It is one of the War's most sublime speeches:*[113]
☞ "Headquarters Forrest's Cavalry Corps, Gainesville, Ala., May 9, 1865. Soldiers, by an agreement made between Lieutenant-General Taylor, commanding the Department of Alabama, Mississippi, and East

Louisiana, and Major-General Canby, commanding United States forces, the troops of this department have been surrendered.

"I do not think it proper or necessary at this time to refer to causes which have reduced us to this extremity; nor is it now a matter of material consequence to us how such results were brought about. That we are beaten is a self-evident fact, and any further resistance on our part would justly be regarded as the very height of folly and rashness.

"The armies of Generals Lee and Johnson having surrendered, you are the last of all the troops of the Confederate States Army east of the Mississippi River to lay down your arms.

"The Cause for which you have so long and so manfully struggled, and for which you have braved dangers, endured privations, and sufferings, and made so many sacrifices, is today hopeless. The government which we sought to establish and perpetuate, is at an end. Reason dictates and humanity demands that no more blood be shed. Fully realizing and feeling that such is the case, it is your duty and mine to lay down our arms, submit to the 'powers that be,' and to aid in restoring peace and establishing law and order throughout the land.

"The terms upon which you were surrendered are favorable, and should be satisfactory and acceptable to all. They manifest a spirit of magnanimity and liberality, on the part of the Federal authorities, which should be met, on our part, by a faithful compliance with all the stipulations and conditions therein expressed. As your Commander, I sincerely hope that every officer and soldier of my command will cheerfully obey the orders given, and carry out in good faith all the terms of the cartel.

"Those who neglect the terms and refuse to be paroled, may assuredly expect, when arrested, to be sent North and imprisoned. Let those who are absent from their commands, from whatever cause, report at once to this place, or to Jackson, Mississippi; or, if too remote from either, to the nearest United States post or garrison, for parole.

"Civil war, such as you have just passed through naturally engenders feelings of animosity, hatred, and revenge. It is our duty to divest ourselves of all such feelings; and as far as it is in our power to do so, to cultivate friendly feelings towards those with whom we have so long contended, and heretofore so widely, but honestly, differed. Neighborhood feuds, personal animosities, and private differences should be blotted out; and, when you return home, a manly, straightforward course of conduct will secure the respect of your enemies. Whatever your responsibilities may be to Government, to society, or to individuals, meet them like men.

"The attempt made to establish a separate and independent Confederation has failed; but the consciousness of having done your duty faithfully, and to the end, will, in some measure, repay for the hardships you have undergone.

"In bidding you farewell, rest assured that you carry with you my best wishes for your future welfare and happiness. Without, in any way, referring to the merits of the Cause in which we have been engaged, your courage and determination, as exhibited on many hard-fought fields, has elicited the respect and admiration of friend and foe. And I now cheerfully and gratefully acknowledge my indebtedness to the officers and men of my command whose zeal, fidelity and unflinching bravery have been the great source of my past success in arms.

The smouldering ruins of the beautiful city of Richmond, Virginia, as it looked after Lincoln and his illegal invaders finished with it in April 1865. Note the cavalry horses reined off along the lower fence.

"I have never, on the field of battle, sent you where I was unwilling to go myself; nor would I now advise you to a course which I felt myself unwilling to pursue. You have been good soldiers, you can be good citizens. Obey the laws, preserve your honor, and the Government to which you have surrendered can afford to be, and will be, magnanimous."[114]

Forrest's men in hand-to-hand combat with Yankee troops.

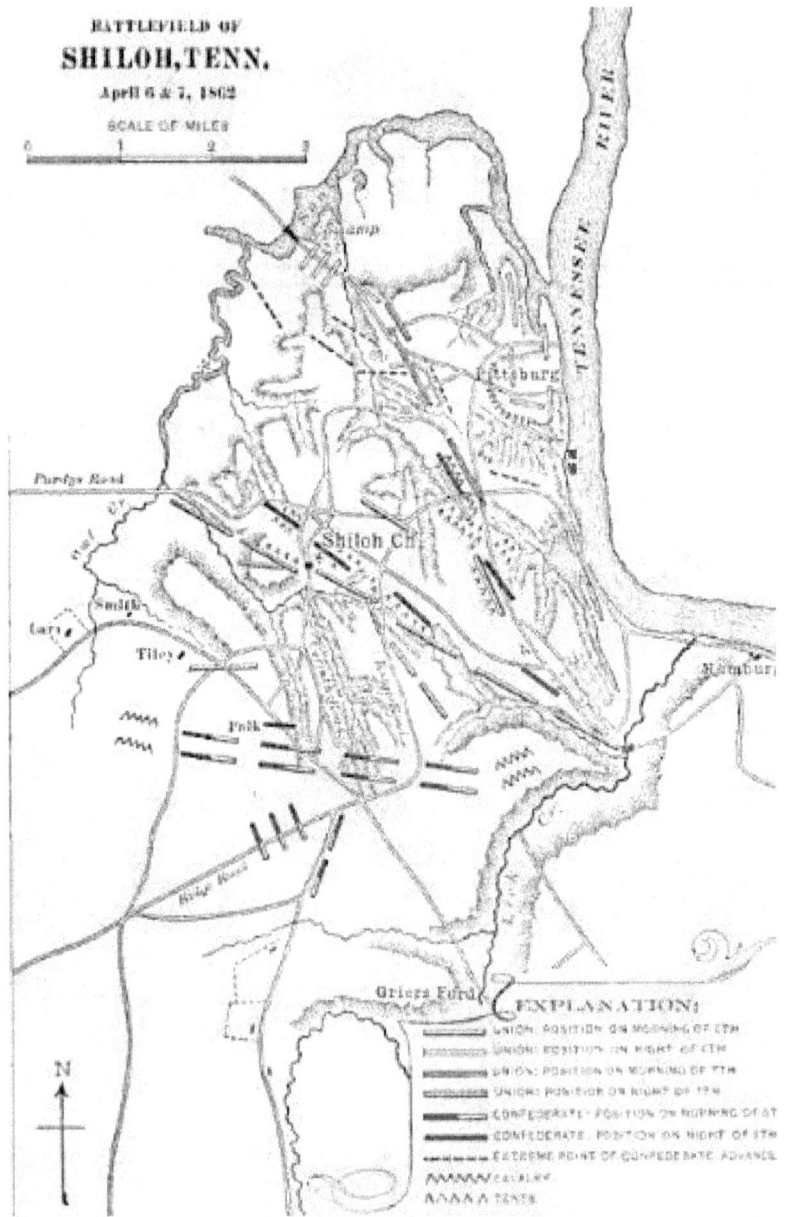

An old map of the Battle of Shiloh, April 6-7, 1862. The Confederates lost, but Forrest, then a colonel, delayed the Union victory by forcing Yankee troops back to Pittsburg Landing.

# SECTION THREE

# POSTBELLUM PERIOD

# YANKEE NEWSPAPER INTERVIEW
## 1868

In the Summer of 1868 Forrest was interviewed by the Cincinnati *Commercial*, after which the piece ran in the August 28, 1868, edition. It might seem strange that Forrest would accept such a request, for he knew better than anyone not to allow a crafty Yankee journalist to question him.

However, at the time he was sincerely interested in trying to repair the damage done to his reputation by Lincoln's anti-South propaganda machine and the cunning Northern press—which was always ready and willing to cook up a scandalous story to make Forrest and the South look bad. Thus, hoping for the best, the General agreed to the interview.

As it turns out, he should have refused, for much of what he said was taken out of context, then rewritten for a Northern audience only interested in reading the latest gossip on "that Devil Forrest." We can not always be sure then which of the following words are actually Forrest's and which are the reporter's.

*When the reporter asked the General how he was dealing with his postwar parole, he replied:*

☞ "Well, sir, when I surrendered my seven thousand men in 1865, I accepted a parole honestly, and have observed it faithfully up to to-day. I have counseled peace in all the speeches I have made. I have advised my people to submit to the laws of the State, oppressive as they are, and unconstitutional as I believe them to be. I was paroled and not pardoned until the issuance of the last proclamation of general amnesty; and, therefore, did not think it prudent for me to take any active part until the oppression of my people became so great that they could not endure it, and then I would be with them. My friends thought differently, and [in July of 1868] sent me to New York [to be a delegate in the Democratic Convention], and I am glad I went there."[115]

Nathan Bedford Forrest as he looked in 1868, three years after Lincoln's War. According to the North's illicit and needlessly cruel Reconstruction policies, he was still considered a "prisoner on parole," guilty of "treason" against the U.S. government.

*Concerning the so-called "Reconstruction" policies of the North, Forrest made this comment:*

☞ ". . . it is growing worse hourly, yet I have said to the people, 'Stand fast, let us try to right the wrong by legislation.' A few weeks ago I was called to Nashville to counsel with other gentlemen who had been prominently identified with the cause of the confederacy, and we then offered pledges which we thought would be satisfactory to [the liberal anti-South Tennessee governor] Mr. Brownlow and his legislature, and we told them that, if they would not call out the militia, we would agree to preserve order and see that the laws were enforced. The legislative committee certainly led me to believe that our proposition would be accepted and no militia organized. Believing this, I came home, and advised all of my people to remain peaceful, and to offer no resistance to any reasonable law. It is true that I never have recognized the present [liberal Yankee imposed] government in Tennessee as having any legal existence, yet I was willing to submit to it for a time, with the hope that the wrongs might be righted peaceably."[116]

*When the Yankee reporter asked Forrest: "What are your feelings toward the*

*Federal Government, general?", he replied:*
☞ "I loved the old [antebellum] Government in 1861; I love the old Constitution yet. I think it the best government in the world if administered as it was before the war. I do hot hate it; I am opposing now only the radical revolutionists [that is, Northern liberals] who are trying to destroy it. I believe that party to be composed, as I know it is in Tennessee, of the worst men on God's earth—men who would hesitate at no crime, and who have only one object in view, to enrich themselves."[117]

*The reporter then asked Forrest: "In the event of Governor Brownlow's calling out the militia, do you think there will be any resistance offered to their acts?", to which the General replied:*
☞ "That will depend upon circumstances. If the militia are simply called out, and do not interfere with or molest any one, I do not think there will be any fight. If, on the contrary, they do what I believe they will do, commit outrages, or oven one outrage, upon the people, they and Mr. Brownlow's government will be swept out of existence; not a radical [that is, an anti-South liberal] will be left alive. If the militia are called out, we cannot but look upon it as a declaration of war, because Mr. Brownlow has already issued his proclamation directing them to shoot down the Ku-Klux wherever they find them; and he [wrongly and unfairly] calls all Southern men Ku Klux."[118]

*When the reporter asked Forrest if there would indeed be a conflict if Brownlow called out his militia against the law-abiding citizens of Tennessee, he said:*
☞ "Yes, sir; if they attempt to carry out Governor Brownlow's proclamation, by shooting down Ku-Klux—for he calls all Southern men Ku-Klux—if they go to hunting down and shooting these men, there will be war, and a bloodier one than we have ever witnessed. I have told these [anti-South liberal] radicals here what they might expect in such an event. I have no powder to burn killing negroes. I intend to kill the radicals [that is, white liberals]. I have told them this and more. There is not a radical [liberal] leader in this town but is a marked man; and if a trouble should break out, not one of them would be left alive. I have told them that they were trying to create a disturbance and then slip out and leave the consequences to fall upon the negro; but they can't do it.

Their houses are picketed, and when the fight comes not one of them would ever get out of this town alive. We don't intend they shall ever get out of the country. But I want it distinctly understood that I am opposed to any war, and will only fight in self defense. If the militia attack us, we will resist to the last; and, if necessary, I think I could raise 40,000 men in five days ready for the field."[119]

*When asked by the reporter if he thought the original Ku Klux Klan (as opposed to the modern KKK, with which it has no connection)[120] was of any benefit to the state of Tennessee, Forrest said:*
☞ "No doubt of it. Since its organization, the [Yankee-formed anti-South] leagues have quit killing and murdering our people. There were some foolish young men who put masks on their faces and rode over the country, frightening negroes; but orders have been issued to stop that, and it has ceased. You may say, further, that three members of the Ku-Klux have been court-martialed and shot for violations of the orders not to disturb or molest people."[121]

*When the reporter asked Forrest if he was a member of the KKK, he replied:*
☞ "I am not; but am in sympathy and will cooperate with them. I know they are charged with many crimes that they are not guilty of."[122]

*When questioned about negro suffrage, Forrest responded:*
☞ "If the negroes vote to enfranchise us, I do not think I would favor their disfranchisement. We will stand by those who help us. And here I want you to understand distinctly I am not an enemy to the negro. We want him here among us; he is the only laboring class we have; and, more than that, I would sooner trust him than the white scalawag [a white anti-South Southerner] or

Lieutenant John Eaton of Forrest's Escort.

carpet-bagger [a white anti-South Northerner]. When I entered the army I took forty-seven negroes into the army with me, and forty-five of them were surrendered with me. I said to them at the start: 'This fight is against slavery; if we lose it, you will be made free; if we whip the fight, and you stay with me and be good boys, I will set you free; in either case you will be free.' These boys staid with me, drove my teams, and better confederates did not live."[123]

*When the reporter asked Forrest: "What do you think is the effect of the [Reconstruction] amnesty granted to your people?", he replied:*
☞ "I believe that the amnesty restored all the rights to the people, full and complete. I do not think the [U.S.] Federal Government has the right to disfranchise any man, but I believe that the legislatures of the States have. The objection I have to the disfranchisement in Tennessee is, that the legislature which enacted the law had no constitutional existence, and the law in itself is a nullity. Still I would respect it until changed by law. But there is a limit beyond which men cannot be driven, and I am ready to die sooner than sacrifice my honor. This thing [Reconstruction] must have an end, and it is now about time for that end to come."[124]

*When asked what he thought of Yankee General Ulysses S. Grant, Forrest replied:*
☞ "I regard him as a great military commander, a good man, honest and liberal, and if elected [to the office of U.S. president] will, I hope and believe, execute the laws honestly and faithfully. And by the way, a report has been published in some of the newspapers, stating that while General Grant and lady were at Corinth, in 1862, they took and carried off furniture and other property. I here brand the author as a liar. I was at Corinth only a short time ago, and I personally investigated the whole matter, talked with the people with whom he and his lady lived while there, and they say that their conduct was everything that could have been expected of a gentleman and lady, and deserving the highest praise. I am opposed to General Grant in everything, but I would do him justice."[125]

*The reporter closed his interview with Forrest with these personal words:*

The foregoing is the principal part of my conversation with the general. I give the conversation, and leave the reader to form his own opinion as to what General Forrest means to do. I think he has been so plain in his talk that it cannot be misunderstood.[126]

*After reading the published interview a few days later, Forrest was not happy. His words had either been misconstrued, or, more likely, intentionally twisted to present him in a false and negative light. Understandably annoyed, Forrest fired off the following barely polite letter to the reporter who had interviewed him:*
☞ "Memphis, September 3, 1868. Dear Sir: I have just read your letter in the [Cincinnati] *Commercial*, giving a report of our conversation on Friday last. I do not think you would intentionally misrepresent me, but you have done so, and, I suppose, because you mistook my meaning. The portions of your letter to which I object are corrected in the following paragraphs:

General Forrest had much in common with the author's cousin, daring Confederate cavalryman and raider John S. Mosby, pictured here (sitting in the center with the plumed hat) with some of his men. The author's fifth great-grandmother is Elizabeth Bacon Mosby, John's second cousin.

"I promise the legislature my personal influence and aid in maintaining order and enforcing the laws. I have never advised the people to resist any law, but to submit to the laws, until they can be corrected by lawful legislation.

"I said the militia bill would occasion no trouble, unless they violated the law by carrying out the governor's proclamation, which I believe to be unconstitutional and in violence of law, in shooting men down without trial, as recommended by that proclamation.

"I said it was reported, and I believed the report, that there are forty thousand Ku-Klux in Tennessee; and I believe the organization stronger in other States. I meant to imply, when I said that the Ku-Klux recognize the Federal Government, that they would obey all State laws. They recognize all laws, and will obey them, so I have been informed, in protecting peaceable citizens from oppression from any quarter.

"I did not say that any man's house was picketed. I did not mean to convey the idea that I would raise any troops; and, more than that, no man could do it in five days, even if they were organized.

"I said that General Grant was at Holly Springs, and not at Corinth; I said the charge against him was false, but did not use the word 'liar.'

"I cannot consent to remain silent in this matter; for, if I did so, under an incorrect impression of my personal views, I might be looked upon as one desiring a conflict, when, in truth, I am so adverse to anything of the kind that I will make any honorable sacrifice to avoid it.

"Hoping that I may have this explanation placed before your readers, I remain, very respectfully, N. B. Forrest."[127]

This 19th-Century illustration shows Forrest's successful raid on Memphis, Tennessee, on August 21, 1864. We Southerners still discuss such engagements as if they happened yesterday.

# JOINT SELECT COMMITTEE INTERROGATION
## 1871

In 1871 the end of Reconstruction still lay six years in the future, and the Northern desire to humiliate Forrest was stronger than ever. As such, on June 27, 1871, he was hauled before a hostile panel of Yankees in Washington, D.C. Known as the "Joint Select Committee on the Condition of Affairs in the Late Insurrectionary States," the nosey meddling Northerners severely grilled the General for several hours in an attempt to trick him into saying something "treasonous." The always clever Forrest, still cruelly and illegally considered a "prisoner on parole," deftly fielded their repetitive, guileful, and often impudent questions, as the following excerpts from the interrogation reveal.

General Forrest and his signature.

*When asked what type of organization the KKK was, Forrest answered:*
☞ ". . . this was a sort of offset [outgrowth] gotten up against the Loyal Leagues [Yankee groups that were inculcating freed blacks with anti-South propaganda and inciting them to violence against white Southerners]."[128]

*When pressed as to the purpose of the KKK, Forrest said:*
☞ "I think it was for self-protection. . . . I think that organization arose about the time the [Yankee Reconstruction] militia were called out, and the [liberal Tennessee] Governor [William G.] Brownlow issued his proclamation stating that the troops would not be injured for what they should do to rebels; such a proclamation was issued. There was a great deal of insecurity felt by the Southern people. There were a great many northern men coming down there, forming leagues all over the country. The negroes were holding night meetings; were going about; were becoming very insolent; and the Southern people all over the State were very much alarmed. I think many of the organizations did not have any name; parties organized themselves so as to be ready in case they were attacked. Ladies were ravished [sexually assaulted] by some of these negroes, who were tried and put in the penitentiary, but were turned out in a few days afterward. There was a great deal of insecurity in the country, and I think this organization was got up to protect the weak, with no political intention at all."[129]

*When asked about any murders that might have taken place under the auspices of the KKK, Forrest alluded to the well-known fact across the South that both whites and blacks were members of the KKK (there was even an all-black KKK chapter in Nashville at the time)*[130]:
☞ "Well, yes, sir; there were men killed in Tennessee and in Mississippi by bands in disguise. There were [KKK] men found down there disguised, white men and negroes both."[131]

*When asked what the purpose of the KKK's Constitution was, Forrest responded:*
☞ "The purport of that constitution, as far as I recollect it now, was that the organization was formed for self-protection. The first obligation they took, if I recollect it aright, was to abide by and obey the laws of the country; to protect the weak; to protect the women and children; obligating themselves to stand by each other in case of insurrection or anything of that sort. I think that was about the substance of the obligation."[132]

*Forrest comments on the deluge of mail he daily received after Lincoln's War:*
☞ "I was getting at that time from fifty to one hundred letters a day,

and had a private secretary writing all the time. I was receiving letters from all the Southern States, men complaining, being dissatisfied, persons whose friends had been killed, or their families insulted, and they were writing to me to know what they ought to do."[133]

*When the Yankee panel asked Forrest what his intentions were toward the KKK, he answered:*
☞ "All my efforts were addressed to stop it, disband it, and prevent it . . . I was trying to keep it down as much as possible."[134]

John Milton Hubbard rode with Forrest, and in 1911 wrote a delightful book about his experiences called *Notes of a Private.*

*When Forrest was asked if he was trying to suppress the many "outrages" then being committed by blacks, Forrest said:*
☞ "By all people; my object was to keep peace."[135]

*When Forrest was asked how he managed to finally "suppress" the KKK, he said:*
☞ "I talked with different people that I believed were connected with it, and urged its disbandment, that it should be broken up."[136]

*When Forrest was asked who the KKK had operated against, he answered:*
☞ "I do not think it operated against any person particularly; I think it was, as I said before, an organization for the protection of Southern people against mobs, and rapes, and things of that sort. I never knew any portion of the organization to commit any deed."[137]

*When asked what he thought of a Yankee-slanted anti-South newspaper article that appeared in the Cincinnati* Commercial *on September 1, 1868, he replied:*
☞ "There were a great many things said in regard to myself that I looked upon as gotten up merely to affect the elections in the North. I

felt that was the object of it."¹³⁸

*Forrest was asked again what the purpose of the KKK was, to which he answered:*
☞ "According to my understanding, the organization was intended entirely as a protection to the people, to enforce the laws, and protect the people against outrages."¹³⁹

*When he was asked why he disbanded the KKK in 1868, Forrest said:*
☞ "[for the reasons that] . . . there was no further use for it; that the country was safe; that there was no apprehension of any trouble."¹⁴⁰

*Completely contrary to Northern myth, Forrest was a friend of African-Americans, not their enemy. Not only did he free* all *of his slaves either before or during Lincoln's War, he happily hired hundreds of free blacks afterward, as he states in the following answer to the Joint Select Committee. He is speaking here of the 400 freedmen he employed on his railroad. The panel asked Forrest if his black workers were allowed to "vote as they please," insinuating that Southerners like the General were forcing their black employees to vote Democratic (then the conservative party):*
☞ "They voted as they pleased at the last election. About three hundred had come from North Carolina, but they were not entitled to vote; had not been in Alabama long enough; they had been working a portion of the time in Mississippi, and they did not vote. But all those who were entitled to vote voted without any molestation. I said when I started out with my roads that railroads had no politics; that I wanted the assistance of everybody; that railroads were for the general good of the whole country. We have had no political discussion along the line of my road; we have had no difficulty. I hired three hundred colored men in North Carolina, and they worked for me twelve months; their time was out last May; they were paid off. About one hundred and fifty of them returned, and a portion of them, in fact I think about fifteen, have come back. They got one-half of their money monthly until the end of the year, when they were paid off."¹⁴¹

*When he was asked if he had accepted parole after the War, Forrest said:*
☞ "I did, and issued an address when I did accept the parole . . it was published in all your [Yankee] papers. I said to my men that they had

Major Charles S. Severson, Forrest's chief quartermaster.

been good soldiers and could be good citizens; that they should go home and obey the laws of the country. And so far as I know, not one soldier who served under me has been molested for any offense since the war."¹⁴²

*When the panel asked if he still had any regard for the Union, Forrest responded:*
☞ "I have said, and have always said, that there was no time during the war that I would not have been willing to have taken up the old [U.S.] flag with the Northern people and fought any other nation, and given the last drop of blood I had. I have said that, and I say it yet."¹⁴³

*When asked if he had ever opposed giving blacks the right to vote, Forrest said:*
☞ "No, sir. My views in regard to this war are probably different from those of most men. I looked upon it as a war upon slavery when it broke out; I so considered it.¹⁴⁴ [Forrest knew this was not true, but said it only to placate his Yankee inquisitors.] I said to forty-five colored fellows on my plantation that it was a war upon slavery, and that I was going into the army; that if they would go with me, if we got whipped they would be free anyhow, and that if we succeeded and slavery was perpetuated, if they would act faithfully with me to the end of the war, I would set them free. Eighteen months before the war closed I was satisfied that we were going to be defeated, and I gave these forty-five men, or forty-four men of them, their free papers, for fear I might be killed."¹⁴⁵

*Concerning his behavior after the end of the War, Forrest said:*
☞ "When the war closed I looked upon it as an act of Providence, and felt that we ought to submit to it quietly; and I have never done or said

anything that was contrary to the laws that have been enacted."¹⁴⁶

*When pushed further on the question of "Negro suffrage," Forrest said:*
☞ "I advocated the fourteenth and fifteenth amendments before the people, and told our people [that is, white Tennesseans] that they were inevitable and should be accepted."¹⁴⁷

*When Forrest was asked, again, about the purpose of the KKK, he said:*
☞ "[It was] for the purpose of preventing crime, and for the purpose of protecting each other in case of sickness, or anything—preventing disorder."¹⁴⁸

*When asked "who" the KKK was supposed to prevent disorder from, Forrest said:*
☞ "By anybody."¹⁴⁹

*When the panel asked why he could not remember certain facts, names, and figures, Forrest replied:*
☞ ". . . In the last two years I have been very busily engaged. I came out of the war pretty well wrecked. I was in the army four years; was on the front all the time, and was in the saddle more than half my time; and when I came out of the army I was completely used up—shot all to pieces, crippled up, and found myself and my family entirely dependent. I went into the army worth a million and a half of dollars [about $45 million in today's currency], and came out a beggar. I have given all my time since then, so far as was in my power, to try to recover."¹⁵⁰

*When asked if the whites of Tennessee believed that Southern blacks were being stirred up by Yankees after the War to riot against their former owners, Forrest said:*
☞ "[Yes.] During the war our servants remained with us, and behaved very well. When the war was over our servants began to mix with the republicans [the liberals of that day], and they broke off from the Southern people, and were sulky and insolent. There was a general fear throughout the country that there would be an uprising, and that with those men who had stopped among us—those men who came in among us, came there and went to our kitchens and consulted with the negroes—many of them never came about the houses at all. It was

different with me. I carried seven Federal officers home with me, after the war was over, and I rented them plantations, some of my own lands, and some of my neighbors'. In 1866 those seven officers made a crop in my neighborhood. I assisted those men, and found great relief from them. They got me my hands, and they kept my hands engaged for me. . . . I persuaded our people to pursue the same course. These [Yankee] men were all young men, and they made my house their home on Sundays."[151]

*When asked yet again how he "suppressed" the KKK, Forrest said:*
☞ "I wrote a great many letters to people, and counseled them to abstain from all violence, and to be quiet and behave themselves, and let these things take their course."[152]

*When asked if he was a "prominent man" in the Confederate army, Forrest said:*
☞ "I was rather a prominent man in the confederate army; I probably fought more battles than any other man in it; I was before the people probably more than any other man that was in it."[153]

*When the panel asked why postwar Southern whites feared a "negro uprising," Forrest said:*
☞ "For the reason that during the war the negroes remained at home working and were quiet, and were not organized. After the war, they left their homes, traveled all over the country, killed all the stock there was in the country to eat, were

Confederate Lieutenant William Richardson. General Forrest saved Richardson's life at the Battle of Murfreesboro, July 13, 1862. Falsely accused of "spying" by an occupying Union soldier, Richardson was tossed in jail and ordered to be hanged the following morning. Forrest and his troops, however, quickly overran the Federal garrison, after which he freed Richardson and had the lieutenant's Yankee accuser immediately executed.

holding these night meetings, were carrying arms, and were making threats."[154]

*When Forrest was asked if Southern blacks were "suffering from the hands of the white men as many wrongs after the war as before and during the war," Forrest replied:*

☞ "I think more; I do not think they were suffering any during the war."[155]

*Forrest was asked if "the object" of the KKK "was to resist outlawry and punish offenders," to which he answered:*

☞ "Yes, sir; I do not think the people [KKK members] intended to go and violate or wrong any one; but it was to punish those men who were guilty, and who the [U.S.] law would not touch [that is, not punish]; and to defend themselves in case of an attack."[156]

*When pressed to cooperate with the Joint Select Committee, Forrest said:*

☞ "I am disposed to do all I can to try and fetch these troubles to an end. I went into the army as a private, and fought my way up to the rank of lieutenant general. I tried to do my duty as a soldier, and since I have been out of the war I have tried to do my duty as a citizen. I have done more probably than any other man in the South to suppress these difficulties and keep them down. While I have been vilified and abused in the papers, and accused of things I never did while in the army and since, I have no desire to hide anything from you at all. I want this matter settled; I want our country quiet once more; and I want to see our people united and working together harmoniously."[157]

*When asked if if he knew personally of any conflicts between whites and blacks, Forrest said:*

☞ "I will mention one case that occurred in 1868. At Crawfordsville, on the Mobile and Ohio Railroad, the citizens and negroes had a difficulty, and the negroes threatened to burn the town. It was telegraphed up to West Point, forty miles above there, and to Columbus also. I was then on my way to Memphis. When I got to the Mobile road I found these men had got all the trains they could and started down, and I went with them. The negroes were about eight hundred strong, and

Captain Reuben R. Ross served under Forrest in the Maury (Tennessee) Artillery.

were out at the edge of the town; the people of the town had fortified themselves; the negroes had burned one house. When I got there I got the white people together, organized them, and made speeches to them. I told them to be quiet, and we would see if this could be settled. I then got on a horse and rode over to the negroes and made a speech to them. The negroes dispersed and went home, and nothing was done; there was nobody hurt, nobody molested. But they were just on the point where it was liable that fifty or five hundred men would be killed. Those negroes had fallen out [that is, gotten upset] with a young [white] man who was going down the road; his horse had got scared when they came along, had kicked out a little, and run against their trumpeter and knocked him down. They followed him into town to beat him, and then they gathered together. I am satisfied I prevented bloodshed there by getting those men together and talking to them, and by talking to the negroes and getting them to go home."[158]

When he was asked, "In the event of a war of races down there [in Tennessee], do you not think the excitement would reach North?", Forrest replied:

☞ "I think it would. I think we would find a great many people up here [in the North] who would go down there and help us if we had the worst of it."[159]

(Note: In the end the Join Select Committee found Forrest innocent of any wrongdoing, and they reluctantly allowed him to return to Tennessee.)

# LAST YEARS
## 1866-1877

Forrest's final years were spent trying to rebuild his life, his businesses, and his fortune. While he was never able to attain the financial status of his antebellum years, he was able to procure a home and land and begin farming again. He also became involved in the construction of railroad lines and the campaign to establish equal rights for blacks—the latter something Lincoln spent his entire life trying to block.[160]

*After the War, when Forrest was asked about what he thought of West Point graduates in the Union army, or "West Pinters," as he referred to them, he answered:*
☞ "Whenever I met one of them fellers that fit by note, I generally whipped hell out of him before he got his tune pitched."[161]

*Forrest, like all former Confederate officers, was placed on parole and subject to impromptu arrest and imprisonment for the alleged crime of "treason against the U.S. government." His family and friends begged him to flee the country, to which he replied:*
☞ "This is my country. I am hard at work upon my plantation, and carefully observing the obligations of my parole. If the Federal government does not regard it they will be sorry. I shall not go away."[162]

*On November 25, 1866, a little over a year after the War, Forrest wrote to President Andrew Johnson, asking for a "pardon." As the following words attest, Forrest was acutely conscious of how he was perceived in the North:*
☞ "I'm . . . aware that at this moment I am regarded in large communities, in the North, with great abhorrence, as a detestable monster, ruthless and swift to take life."[163]

In 1870 Forrest got into a disagreement with one of his contractors, a man named Colonel A. K. Shepherd. Shepherd challenged his boss to a dual and the hot-headed Forrest accepted. That night, however, as he lay in bed thinking things over, he began to feel uneasy. Knowing he would certainly kill an innocent man, friend, and business partner, Forrest marched to Shepherd's office the next day, and said:

☞ "Colonel, I am in the wrong in this affair and I have come to say so."[164]

A postwar image of Colonel A. A. Russell, who commanded the Fourth Alabama Cavalry under Forrest.

(Note: Shepherd was elated, the duel was canceled, and another man's life was spared.)

In 1872, now former Confederate Captain John S. Wilkes, met up with Forrest one last time, on this occasion at the Maxwell House Hotel in Nashville, Tennessee. Wilkes had just turned down an offer to be comptroller under Tennessee Governor (and former Confederate General) John Calvin Brown. Forrest approached Wilkes, and shaking his finger at him, said:

☞ "Young man, I thought you was a damned fool at Fort Donelson, and I haven't changed my opinion. You are too damned particular to be a politician."[165]

In order to sabotage Forrest's reputation, embarrass the South, and arouse Yankee hatred of Dixie, the North has long portrayed him as a entrenched racist. To a great extent this ploy has worked. To this day, a majority of people—even in the South—associate Forrest's name with racism. This despite the fact that he was, unlike Lincoln and most other Northerners, not truly prejudiced against those of African descent. To the contrary, he did much to help blacks before and during the War, while working hard to heal the rift between the races afterward.

# The Quotable Nathan Bedford Forrest

*Nowhere are Forrest's real views on race more evident than in a speech he gave at Memphis, Tennessee, on July 4, 1875. His audience was the Independent Order of Pole Bearers, a sociopolitical group of black Southerners (and forerunner of the NAACP). As reported by the unreconstructed Memphis* Daily Avalanche, *July 6, 1875, an African-American woman named Miss Lou Lewis, handed Forrest a bouquet of flowers, "as a token, of reconciliation, an offering of peace and good will." Bowing to the crowd, Forrest said:*

☞ "Miss Lewis, ladies and gentlemen—I accept these flowers as a token of reconciliation between the white and colored races of the South. I accept them more particularly, since they come from a lady, for if there is any one on God's great earth who loves the ladies, it is myself.

"This is a proud day for me. Having occupied the position I have for thirteen years, and being misunderstood by the colored race, I take this occasion to say that I am your friend. I am here as the representative of the Southern people—one that has been more maligned than any other. I assure you that everyman who was in the Confederate army is your friend. We were born on the same soil, breathe the same air, live in the same land, and why should we not be brothers and sisters.

"When the war broke out I believed it to be my duty to fight for my country, and I did so. I came here with the jeers and sneers of a few white people, who did not think it right. I think it is right, and will do all I can to bring about harmony, peace and unity. I want to elevate every man, and to see you take your places in your shops, stores and offices. I don't propose to say anything about politics, but I want you to do as I do—go to the polls and select the best men to vote for. I feel that you are free men, I am a free man, and we can do as we please.

"I came here as a friend, and whenever I can serve any of you I will do so. We have one Union, one flag, one country, therefore let us stand together. Although we differ in color, we should not differ in sentiment.

"Many things have been said in regard to myself, and many reports circulated, which may perhaps be believed by some of you, but there are many around me who can contradict them. I have been many times in the heat of battle—oftener, perhaps, than any within the sound of my voice. Men have come to me to ask for quarter, both black and white, and I have shielded them. Do your duty as citizens, and if any are oppressed, I will be your friend. I thank you for the flowers, and assure you that I am with you in heart and hand."¹⁶⁶

*After Lincoln's War, Forrest was enthusiastically attacked by uninformed Yankees for his role in the so-called "Fort Pillow Massacre." As I make clear in a detailed discussion in my award-winning book* A Rebel Born, *there was no massacre. Just absurd fictions created by the Northern Press in an attempt to stain Forrest's reputation. Forrest did not take the accusations lying down, and used every opportunity to defend himself and his troops. In Jordan and Pryor's great 1868 autobiographical work, the General endorsed the following statement, testifying to the fact that no atrocities occurred at Fort Pillow, and that*

☞ "all allegations to the contrary are mere malicious inventions, started, nurtured, and accredited at a time, and through a sentiment of strong sectional animosity."¹⁶⁷

*Forrest never got over his lack of formal education, stating:*

☞ "No one knows the embarrassment I labor under when thrown in the company of educated persons."¹⁶⁸

Confederate Major John P. Strange, Forrest's assistant adjutant general.

*In his last year of life, 1877, Forrest formally converted to Christianity, an act that had a profound impact on the old war chief. Among other things, he dropped all of his lawsuits, even though his attorneys assured him that they were winnable and that they would have enabled him to recoup most of his financial losses.*¹⁶⁹ *One of his legal advisors, a former Forrest soldier named General John T. Morgan, continued to pressure him to fight for his claims, to which Forrest responded:*

☞ "General, I am broken in spirit and have not long to live. My life has been a battle from the start. It was a fight to achieve a livelihood for those dependent upon me in my younger days, and an independence for myself when I grew up to manhood, as well as in the terrible turmoil of the Civil War. I have seen too much violence, and I want to close my days in peace with all the world, as I am now at peace with my Maker."[170]

*Forrest's final public appearance was on September 21, 1877, at a reunion of the Seventh Tennessee Regiment of Cavalry in Memphis (he had enlisted in the regiment as a private sixteen years earlier, on June 14, 1861).*[171] *From astride his horse he read the following speech, his last one, to the attentive crowd:*

☞ "Soldiers of the Seventh Tennessee Cavalry. Ladies, and Gentlemen: I name the soldiers first because I love them best. I am extremely pleased to meet you here to-day. I love the gallant men with whom I was so intimately connected during the war. You can hardly realize what must pass through a commander's mind when called upon to meet in reunion the brave spirits who, through four years of war and bloodshed, fought fearlessly for a cause that they thought right, and who, even when they foresaw as we did, that the war must soon close in disaster, and that we must all surrender, yet did not quail, but marched to victory in many battles, and fought as boldly and persistently in their last battles as they did in their first. Nor do I forget those many gallant spirits who sleep coldly in death upon the many bloody battle-fields of the late war. I love them too, and honor their memory. I have often been called to the side, on the battle-field, of those who have been struck down, and they would put their arms around my neck, draw me down to them, and kiss me, and say: 'General, I have fought my last battle and will soon be gone. I want you to remember my wife and children and take care of them.' Comrades, I have remembered their wives and little ones, and have taken care of them, and I want everyone of you to remember them too, and join with me in the labor of love.

"Comrades, through the years of bloodshed and weary marches you were tried and true soldiers. So through the years of peace you have been good citizens, and now that we are again united under the old [U.S.] flag, I love it as I did in the days of my youth, and I feel sure that you love it also. Yes, I love and honor that old flag as much as those who followed it on the other side; and I am sure that I but express your feelings when I say that should occasion offer and our country demand our services, you would as eagerly follow my lead to battle under that proud banner as ever you followed me in our late great war. It has been thought by some that our social reunions were wrong, and that they

The author's cousin Emma Sansom of Social Circle, Georgia. On May 2, 1863, the brave fifteen year old led General Forrest to a hidden ford on Black Creek following the Battle of Day's Gap near Gadsden, Alabama. This enabled him to capture Union forces and save the railroad.

would be heralded to the North as an evidence that we were again ready to break out into civil war. But I think that they are right and proper, and we will show our countrymen by our conduct and dignity that brave soldiers are always good citizens and law-abiding and loyal people.

"Soldiers, I was afraid that I could not be with you to-day, but I could not bear the thought of not meeting with you, and I will always try to meet with you in the future. And I hope that you will continue to meet from year to year, and bring your wives and children with you, and let them, and the children who may come after them, enjoy with you the pleasure of your reunions."[172]

*On October 29, 1877, frail, emaciated, and gentle, with "the voice and manner of a woman,"[173] but still possessing his "blazing eyes" and his fiery Anglo-Celtic spirit, a mellowed, silver-haired, white-bearded, fifty-six year old Forrest uttered his last coherent words in Memphis, Tennessee:*

☛ "Call my wife."[174]

*Fifteen minutes later, at 7:15 PM, he died peacefully from exhaustion, high blood pressure related issues,[175] the effects of a spinal wound (received at the Battle of Shiloh), malaria, chronic dysentery and diarrhea, and complications due to diabetes.[176] Nathan Bedford Forrest will live forever in the memory of traditional Southerners and all true lovers of liberty and righteousness.*

# NOTES

1. Seabrook, ARB, p. 330.
2. Wyeth, LGNBF, p. 10.
3. Mathes, p. 12.
4. Seabrook, ARB, p. 202.
5. Mary Ann's father, War of 1812 veteran William H. Montgomery, died at age 37 in 1829, leaving her mother, Elizabeth Cowan, a widow at age 27 (note: William and Elizabeth were 1$^{st}$ cousins). Mary Ann was only three years old at the time. As Elizabeth was now alone and struggling with four young children, her brother Sam took over for William, becoming the family's foster father.
6. Seabrook, ARB, p. 203.
7. Mathes, p. 357. One other time Forrest drank alcohol was in September 1863, and it was certainly not for pleasure. After receiving a wound during his stand at Tunnel Hill (Battle of Chickamauga), his doctor ordered him to drink whiskey to ease the pain.
8. Bradley, p. 135 (quote used by permission of the author).
9. Henry, FWMF, p. 29.
10. Jordan and Pryor, p. 40.
11. The Seventh Tennessee Regiment of Cavalry was one of the last groups of Rebels to surrender at the end of the War in May 1865. Wyeth, LGNBF, pp. 23-24.
12. Mathes, pp. 24, 162. The Confederate States of America never had the funds to properly supply its armies. In particular, while Billy Yank was equipped with the breech-loading rifle, Johnny Reb often had to make do with a shotgun or a squirrel rifle (brought from home), or even the same type of muzzle-loading musket his great-grandfather had used in the Revolutionary War nearly ninety years earlier. That Confederates were proudly fighting America's Second Revolutionary War with the same rifles used in America's First Revolutionary War was an irony not lost on the average Rebel soldier. Wyeth, LGNBF, p. 51.
13. ORA, Ser. 1, Vol. 31, Pt. 3, p. 789. The Confederate government never repaid Forrest for this $20,000, for it was destroyed by Lincoln. Morton, p. 136.
14. *The United Daughters of the Confederacy* magazine, Vols. 56-57, 1993, p. 22.
15. R. Taylor, p. 200.
16. Mathes, p. 37.
17. Mathes, p. 40.
18. Ohio Commandery, p. 81.
19. Wyeth, LGNBF, pp. 50-51.
20. Morton, p. 258.
21. Wyeth, LGNBF, p. 644.
22. Wyeth, LGNBF, p. 33.
23. Morton, p. 196; Wyeth, LGNBF, p. 198; Mathes, p. 116.
24. Wyeth, LGNBF, p. 631.
25. Wyeth, LGNBF, p. 409.
26. Seabrook, ARB, p. 67.
27. Headley, pp. 97-98.
28. Lanier, Vol. 4, p. 282.
29. Mathes, p. 383. Translated from the original Forrestese, the note reads: "I told you twice goddamn it, no!"
30. Wyeth, LGNBF, p. 77.
31. Wyeth, LGNBF, p. 629.
32. Andrews, p. 280.
33. Wyeth, LGNBF, pp. 212-213.
34. Wyeth, LGNBF, pp. 302-303; Morton, pp. 148-149.
35. Forrest had at one time transferred Gould to another command after the young officer had wrongly abandoned two guns on Sand Mountain. Though not meant personally, Gould took it so. Lytle, p. 181.
36. Morton, pp. 102-103.
37. Traditional Forrest anecdote.
38. Wyeth, LGNBF, p. 264.

39. Wyeth, LGNBF, pp. 265-266.
40. Wyeth, LGNBF, p. 266.
41. Wyeth, LGNBF, pp. 135-136.
42. ORA, Ser. 1, Vol. 45, Pt. 1, pp. 759-760.
43. D. M. Bower, "Concerning Commanders," *Journal of the United Service Institution of India*, United Service Institution of India, Vol. 27, 1898, p. 103.
44. Barrow, Segars, and Rosenburg, BC, p. 97.
45. See e.g., Jordan and Pryor, p. 531.
46. See e.g., Henry, ATSF, p. 188.
47. Henry, FWMF, p. 14.
48. ORA, Ser. 1, Vol. 39, Pt. 2, p. 756. See also Jordan and Pryor, p. 556.
49. Wyeth, LGNBF, p. 640.
50. Lincoln's promise of "forty acres and a mule" for freedmen was an outright lie, one he never intended to uphold. It turned out to be nothing but a lure to draw blacks off their plantations in an effort to destroy the South's infrastructure. There were never any mules, and most of his so-called "black land giveaways" ultimately went to rich white Northerners. See Seabrook, EYWTACWW, p. 128; Mullen, p. 33; Rosenbaum and Brinkley, s.v. "Forty Acres and a Mule"; J. H. Franklin, p. 37; Thornton and Ekelund, p. 96.
51. Henry, ATSF, pp. 200-201.
52. ORA, Ser. 1, Vol. 39, Pt. 1, p. 545.
53. Wyeth, LGNBF, p. 151.
54. Jordan and Pryor, p. 247.
55. Morton, p. 88.
56. Wyeth, LGNBF, p. 184.
57. Wyeth, LGNBF, p. 544.
58. Seabrook, ARB, p. 180.
59. Wyeth, LGNBF, p. 580.
60. Maury, p. 209.
61. D. M. Bower, "Concerning Commanders," *Journal of the United Service Institution of India*, United Service Institution of India, Vol. 27, 1898, p. 103.
62. Wyeth, LGNBF, p. 135.
63. ORA, Ser. 1, Vol. 32, Pt. 3, p. 664.
64. ORA, Ser. 1, Vol. 32, Pt. 1, p. 547.
65. Seabook, ARB, p. 327.
66. Hubbard, p. 99.
67. Seabrook, ARB, p. 542.
68. Morton, p. 231.
69. Witherspoon, pp. 68-69.
70. Seabrook, ARB, p. 211.
71. Maury, p. 215.
72. Seabrook, ARB, p. 35.
73. *Trotwood's Monthly, Devoted to Farm, Horse and Home*, Vol. 2, No. 6, September 1906, p. 684 (Nashville, TN).
74. *Trotwood's Monthly, Devoted to Farm, Horse and Home*, Vol. 2, No. 6, September 1906, p. 684 (Nashville, TN).
75. Mathes, p. 51.
76. Wyeth, LGNBF, p. 640.
77. Seabrook, ARB, p. 636.
78. Wyeth, LGNBF, p. 578.
79. J. H. Wilson, p. 217.
80. Morton, p. 316.
81. Morton, p. 317.
82. Website: http://old.nationalreview.com/hanson/hanson040502.asp.

83. For a detailed study of Forrest's wartime military writings, see my book, *Give 'Em Hell Boys! The Complete Military Correspondence of Nathan Bedford Forrest.*
84. ORA, Ser. 1, Vol. 7, pp. 4-6.
85. ORA, Ser. 1, Vol. 7, pp. 64-66.
86. ORA, Ser. 1, Vol. 7, pp. 383-387.
87. ORA, Ser. 1, Vol. 7, pp. 429-431.
88. ORA, Ser. 1, Vol. 16, Pt. 1, pp. 809-811.
89. ORA, Ser. 1, Vol. 23, Pt. 1, p. 121.
90. Sheppard, pp. 306-307.
91. Wyeth, LGNBF, p. 641.
92. Lytle, p. 194.
93. ORA, Ser. 1, Vol. 23, Pt. 2, pp. 955-956; ORA, Ser. 1, Vol. 30, Pt. 4, pp. 508-509.
94. ORA, Ser. 1, Vol. 32, Pt. 1, pp. 354-355.
95. Seabrook, ARB, pp. 310-311.
96. ORA, Ser. 1, Vol. 32, Pt. 1, pp. 365-357.
97. ORA, Ser. 1, Vol. 32, Pt. 3, pp. 663-665.
98. ORA, Ser. 1, Vol. 32, Pt. 1, p. 119.
99. ORA, Ser. 1, Vol. 32, Pt. 1, p. 596. See also Jordan and Pryor, p. 431.
100. ORA, Ser. 1, Vol. 32, Pt. 1, p. 609.
101. ORA, Ser. 1, Vol. 32, Pt. 1, pp. 613-617.
102. ORA, Ser. 1, Vol. 39, Pt. 1, pp. 228-230.
103. ORA, Ser. 1, Vol. 39, Pt. 1, p. 521.
104. ORA, Ser. 1, Vol. 39, Pt. 3, p. 807.
105. ORA, Ser. 1, Vol. 39, Pt. 1, p. 549.
106. ORA, Ser. 1, Vol. 39, Pt. 3, p. 915.
107. Henry, ATSF, pp. 46, 206; Bradley, pp. 118-124; Browning, pp. 23, 25, 27.
108. Wyeth, LGNBF, p. 120.
109. Henry, FWMF, p. 112.
110. ORA, Ser. 1, Vol. 39, Pt. 1, pp. 870-872.
111. Wyeth, LGNBF, p. 578.
112. ORA, Ser. 1, Vol. 49, Pt. 2, pp. 1263-1264.
113. Forrest's speech was not actually given, but was handed out on flyers. Morton, p. 317.
114. ORA, Ser. 1, Vol. 49, Pt. 2, pp. 1289-1290.
115. *Testimony*, Vol. 13, p. 33.
116. *Testimony*, Vol. 13, p. 33.
117. *Testimony*, Vol. 13, p. 33.
118. *Testimony*, Vol. 13, p. 33.
119. *Testimony*, Vol. 13, p. 34.
120. For the truth about the original Southern KKK, see Seabrook, EYWTACWW, pp. 193-195.
121. *Testimony*, Vol. 13, p. 34.
122. *Testimony*, Vol. 13, p. 34.
123. *Testimony*, Vol. 13, p. 34.
124. *Testimony*, Vol. 13, p. 34.
125. *Testimony*, Vol. 13, p. 34.
126. *Testimony*, Vol. 13, p. 34.
127. *Testimony*, Vol. 13, p. 35.
128. *Testimony*, Vol. 13, p. 6.
129. *Testimony*, Vol. 13, pp. 6-7.
130. Seabrook, ARB, p. 441.
131. *Testimony*, Vol. 13, p. 7.
132. *Testimony*, Vol. 13, p. 9.
133. *Testimony*, Vol. 13, p. 9.
134. *Testimony*, Vol. 13, pp. 11, 12.
135. *Testimony*, Vol. 13, p. 12.

136. *Testimony*, Vol. 13, p. 12.
137. *Testimony*, Vol. 13, p. 12.
138. *Testimony*, Vol. 13, p. 13.
139. *Testimony*, Vol. 13, p. 15.
140. *Testimony*, Vol. 13, p. 16.
141. *Testimony*, Vol. 13, p. 17.
142. *Testimony*, Vol. 13, p. 19.
143. *Testimony*, Vol. 13, p. 20.
144. For a full discussion on the true causes behind Lincoln's War, see Seabrook, EYWTACWW, passim.
145. *Testimony*, Vol. 13, p. 20.
146. *Testimony*, Vol. 13, p. 20.
147. *Testimony*, Vol. 13, p. 20.
148. *Testimony*, Vol. 13, p. 23.
149. *Testimony*, Vol. 13, p. 23.
150. *Testimony*, Vol. 13, p. 24.
151. *Testimony*, Vol. 13, p. 24.
152. *Testimony*, Vol. 13, p. 27.
153. *Testimony*, Vol. 13, p. 28.
154. *Testimony*, Vol. 13, p. 28.
155. *Testimony*, Vol. 13, p. 29.
156. *Testimony*, Vol. 13, p. 29.
157. *Testimony*, Vol. 13, p. 30.
158. *Testimony*, Vol. 13, p. 31.
159. *Testimony*, Vol. 13, p. 31.
160. For more on liberal Lincoln's racist treatment of African-Americans, see my books, *Abraham Lincoln: The Southern View*; *Lincolnology: The Real Abraham Lincoln Revealed in His Own Words*; *The Unquotable Abraham Lincoln*; and *Everything You Were Taught About the Civil War is Wrong, Ask a Southerner!*
161. Morton, pp. 12-13.
162. Wyeth, LGNBF, p. 617.
163. Seabrook, ARB, p. 159.
164. Seabrook, ARB, pp. 482-483.
165. *Trotwood's Monthly, Devoted to Farm, Horse and Home*, Vol. 2, No. 6, September 1906, p. 684 (Nashville, TN).
166. Seabrook, ARB, pp. 459-460.
167. Jordan and Pryor, p. 440.
168. Wyeth, LGNBF, p. 627.
169. Wyeth, LGNBF, p. 623.
170. Wyeth, LGNBF, p. 622.
171. At the time the Seventh Tennessee was known as White's Tennessee Mounted Rifles. Wyeth, LGNBF, p. 23.
172. Mathes, pp. 374-376.
173. Wyeth, LGNBF, p. 621.
174. Traditional Southern anecdote.
175. Bradley, p. 138.
176. Henry, FWMF, p. 459.

# BIBLIOGRAPHY

Andrews, Matthew Page. *The Women of the South in War Times*. Baltimore, MD: Norman, Remington Co., 1920.
Barrow, Charles Kelly, J. H. Segars, and R. B. Rosenburg (eds.). *Black Confederates*. 1995. Gretna, LA: Pelican Publishing Co., 2001 ed.
———. *Forgotten Confederates: An Anthology About Black Southerners*. Saint Petersburg, FL: Southern Heritage Press, 1997.
Bradley, Michael R. *Nathan Bedford Forrest's Escort and Staff*. Gretna, LA: Pelican Publishing Co., 2006.
Browning, Robert, M., Jr. *Forrest: The Confederacy's Relentless Warrior*. Dulles, VA: Brassey's, Inc., 2004.
Franklin, John Hope. *Reconstruction After the Civil War*. Chicago, IL: University of Chicago Press, 1961.
Headley, John W. *Confederate Operations in New York and Canada*. New York, NY: Neale Publishing Co., 1906.
Henry, Robert Selph. *The Story of the Confederacy*. 1931. New York, NY: Konecky and Konecky, 1999 ed.
———. (ed.). *As They Saw Forrest: Some Recollections and Comments of Contemporaries*. 1956. Wilmington, NC: Broadfoot Publishing Co., 1991 ed.
———. *First with the Most: Forrest*. New York, NY: Konecky and Konecky, 1992.
Hopkins, Luther W. *From Bull Run to Appomattox: A Boy's View*. Baltimore, MD: Fleet-McGinley Co., 1914.
Hubbard, John Milton. *Notes of a Private*. Memphis, TN: E. H. Clarke and Brother, 1909.
Jordan, Thomas, and John P. Pryor. *The Campaigns of General Nathan Bedford Forrest and of Forrest's Cavalry*. New Orleans, LA: Blelock and Co., 1868.
Lanier, Robert S. (ed.). *The Photographic History of the Civil War*. 10 vols. New York, NY: Review of Reviews Co., 1911.
Lytle, Andrew Nelson. *Bedford Forrest and His Critter Company*. New York, NY: G. P. Putnam's Sons, 1931.
Mathes, Capt. J. Harvey. *General Forrest*. New York, NY: D. Appleton and Co., 1902.
Maury, Dabney Herndon. *Recollections of a Virginian in the Mexican, Indian, and Civil Wars*. New York, NY: Charles Scribner's Sons, 1894.
Morton, John Watson. *The Artillery of Nathan Bedford Forrest's Cavalry*. Nashville, TN: The M. E. Church, 1909.
Mullen, Robert W. *Blacks in America's Wars: The Shift in Attitudes from the Revolutionary War to Vietnam*. 1973. New York, NY: Pathfinder, 1991 ed.
Ohio Commandery. *Sketches of War History, 1861-1865: Papers Read Before the Ohio Commandery of the Military Order of the Loyal Legion of the United States, 1883-1886* (Vol. 1). Cincinnati, OH: Robert Clarke and Co., 1888.
ORA (full title: *The War of the Rebellion: A Compilation of the Official Records of the Union and Confederate Armies*. (Multiple volumes.) Washington, D.C.: Government Printing Office, 1880.
Rosenbaum, Robert A., and Douglas Brinkley (eds.). *The Penguin Encyclopedia of American History*. New York, NY: Viking, 2003.

Seabrook, Lochlainn. *Carnton Plantation Ghost Stories: True Tales of the Unexplained From Tennessee's Most Haunted Civil War House!* 2005. Franklin, TN: Sea Raven Press, 2011 ed.

———. *Nathan Bedford Forrest: Southern Hero, American Patriot: Honoring a Confederate Hero and the Old South.* 2007. Franklin, TN: Sea Raven Press, 2010 ed.

———. *Abraham Lincoln: The Southern View - Demythologizing America's Sixteenth President.* 2007. Franklin, TN: Sea Raven Press, 2010 ed.

———. *The McGavocks of Carnton Plantation: A Southern History - Celebrating One of Dixie's Most Noble Confederate Families and Their Tennessee Home.* 2008. Franklin, TN: Sea Raven Press, 2011 ed.

———. *A Rebel Born: A Defense of Nathan Bedford Forrest.* 2010. Franklin, TN: Sea Raven Press, 2011 ed.

———. *Everything You Were Taught About the Civil War is Wrong, Ask a Southerner! - Correcting the Errors of Yankee "History."* Franklin, TN: Sea Raven Press, 2010.

———. *Lincolnology: The Real Abraham Lincoln Revealed in His Own Words - A Study of Lincoln's Suppressed, Misinterpreted, and Forgotten Writings and Speeches.* Franklin, TN: Sea Raven Press, 2011.

———. *The Quotable Jefferson Davis: Selections From the Writings and Speeches of the Confederacy's First President.* Franklin, TN: Sea Raven Press, 2011.

———. *The Unquotable Abraham Lincoln: The President's Quotes They Don't Want You to Know!* Franklin, TN: Sea Raven Press, 2011.

———. *The Quotable Robert E. Lee: Selections From the Writings and Speeches of the South's Most Beloved Civil War General.* Franklin, TN: Sea Raven Press, 2011.

———. *Give 'Em Hell Boys! The Complete Military Correspondence of Nathan Bedford Forrest.* Franklin, TN: Sea Raven Press, 2012.

Sheppard, Eric William. *Bedford Forrest, The Confederacy's Greatest Cavalryman.* 1930. Dayton, OH: Morningside House, 1981 ed.

Taylor, Richard. *Destruction and Reconstruction: Personal Experiences of the Late War in the United States.* New York, NY: D. Appleton, 1879.

*Testimony Taken By the Joint Select Committee to Inquire Into the Condition of Affairs in the Late Insurrectionary States.* 13 vols. Washington, D.C.: Government Printing Office, 1872.

Thornton, Mark, and Robert B. Ekelund, Jr. *Tariffs, Blockades, and Inflation: The Economics of the Civil War.* Wilmington, DE: Scholarly Resources, 2004.

Warner, Ezra J. *Generals in Gray: Lives of the Confederate Commanders.* 1959. Baton Rouge, LA: Louisiana State University Press, 1989 ed.

———. *Generals in Blue: Lives of the Union Commanders.* 1964. Baton Rouge, LA: Louisiana State University Press, 2006 ed.

Wilson, James Harrison. *Under the Old Flag: Recollections of Military Operations in the War for the Union, the Spanish War the Boxer Rebellion, Etc.* New York, NY: D. Appleton and Co., 1912.

Witherspoon, William. *Reminiscences of a Scout, Spy and Soldier of Forrest's Cavalry.* Jackson, TN: McCowat Mercer Printing Co., 1910.

Wyeth, John Allan. *Life of General Nathan Bedford Forrest.* New York, NY: Harper and Brothers, 1899.

# MEET THE AUTHOR

LOCHLAINN SEABROOK, winner of the Jefferson Davis Historical Gold Medal for his "masterpiece," *A Rebel Born: A Defense of Nathan Bedford Forrest,* is an unreconstructed Southern historian, award-winning author, Forrest scholar, and traditional Southern Agrarian of Scottish, English, Irish, Welsh, German, and Italian extraction. An encyclopedist, lexicographer, musician, artist, graphic designer, genealogist, and photographer, as well as an award-winning poet, songwriter, and screenwriter, he has a thirty year background in historical nonfiction writing and is a member of the Sons of Confederate Veterans, the Civil War Trust, and the Grange.

(Illustration © Tracy Latham)

Due to similarities in their writing styles, ideas, and literary works, Seabrook is referred to as the "American ROBERT GRAVES," after his cousin, the prolific English writer, historian, mythographer, poet, and author of the classic tomes *The White Goddess* and *The Greek Myths.*

The grandson of an Appalachian coal-mining family, Seabrook is a seventh-generation Kentuckian, co-chair of the Jent/Gent Family Committee (Kentucky), founder and director of the Blakeney Family Tree Project, and a board member of the Friends of Colonel Benjamin E. Caudill. Seabrook's literary works have been endorsed by leading authorities, museum curators, award-winning historians, bestselling authors, celebrities, noted scientists, well respected educators, renown military artists, esteemed Southern organizations, and distinguished academicians from around the world.

As a professional writer Seabrook has authored some thirty popular adult books specializing in the following topics: the American Civil War, pro-South studies, Confederate biography and history, the anthropology of religion, genealogical monographs, Goddess-worship (thealogy), ghost stories, the paranormal, family histories, military encyclopedias, etymological dictionaries, ufology, social issues, comparative analysis of the origins of Christmas, and cross-cultural studies of the family and marriage.

Seabrook's seven children's books include a dictionary of religion and myth, a rewriting of the King Arthur legend (which reinstates the original pre-Christian motifs), two bedtime stories for preschoolers, a naturalist's guidebook to owls, a worldwide look at the family, and an examination of the

Near-Death Experience.

Of blue-blooded Southern stock through his Kentucky, Tennessee, Virginia, West Virginia, and North Carolina ancestors, he is a direct descendant of European royalty via his 6$^{th}$ great-grandfather, the EARL OF OXFORD, after which London's famous Harley Street is named. Among his celebrated male Celtic ancestors is ROBERT THE BRUCE, King of Scotland, Seabrook's 22$^{nd}$ great-grandfather. The 21$^{st}$ great-grandson of EDWARD I "LONGSHANKS" PLANTAGENET), King of England, Seabrook is a thirteenth-generation Southerner through his descent from the colonists of Jamestown, Virginia (1607).

The 2$^{nd}$, 3$^{rd}$, and 4$^{th}$ great-grandson of dozens of Confederate soldiers, one of his closest connections to the War for Southern Independence is through his 3$^{rd}$ great-grandfather, ELIAS JENT, SR., who fought for the Confederacy in the Thirteenth Cavalry Kentucky under Seabrook's 2$^{nd}$ cousin, Colonel BENJAMIN E. CAUDILL. The Thirteenth, also known as "Caudill's Army," fought in numerous conflicts, including the Battles of Saltville, Gladsville, Mill Cliff, Poor Fork, Whitesburg, and Leatherwood.

Seabrook is also related to the following Confederates and other 19$^{th}$-Century luminaries: ROBERT E. LEE, STEPHEN DILL LEE, JOHN SINGLETON MOSBY, STONEWALL JACKSON, NATHAN BEDFORD FORREST, JAMES LONGSTREET, JOHN HUNT MORGAN, JEB STUART, P. G. T. BEAUREGARD (designed the Confederate Battle Flag), JOHN BELL HOOD, ALEXANDER PETER STEWART, ARTHUR M. MANIGAULT, JOSEPH MANIGAULT, EDMUND W. PETTUS, JOHN B. WOMACK, THEODRICK "TOD" CARTER, CHARLES SCOTT VENABLE, THORNTON A. WASHINGTON, JOHN A. WASHINGTON, JOHN H. WINDER, GIDEON J. PILLOW, STATES RIGHTS GIST, EDMUND WINCHESTER RUCKER, HENRY R. JACKSON, JOHN C. BRECKINRIDGE, LEONIDAS POLK, ZACHARY TAYLOR, SARAH KNOX TAYLOR (the first wife of

(Photo © Lochlainn Seabrook)

JEFFERSON DAVIS), RICHARD TAYLOR, DAVY CROCKETT, DANIEL BOONE, MERIWETHER LEWIS (of the Lewis and Clark Expedition) ANDREW JACKSON, JAMES K. POLK, ABRAM POINDEXTER MAURY (founder of Franklin, TN), WILLIAM GILES HARDING, ZEBULON VANCE, THOMAS JEFFERSON, GEORGE WYTHE RANDOLPH (grandson of Jefferson), FELIX K. ZOLLICOFFER, FITZHUGH LEE, NATHANIEL F. CHEAIRS, JESSE JAMES, FRANK JAMES, ROBERT BRANK VANCE, CHARLES SIDNEY WINDER, JOHN W. MCGAVOCK, CARRIE (WINDER)

# THE QUOTABLE NATHAN BEDFORD FORREST  127

MCGAVOCK, DAVID HARDING MCGAVOCK, LYSANDER MCGAVOCK, JAMES RANDAL MCGAVOCK, RANDAL WILLIAM MCGAVOCK, FRANCIS MCGAVOCK, EMILY MCGAVOCK, WILLIAM HENRY F. LEE, LUCIUS E. POLK, MINOR MERIWETHER (husband of noted pro-South author Elizabeth Avery Meriwether), ELLEN BOURNE TYNES (wife of Forrest's chief of artillery, Captain John W. Morton), South Carolina Senators PRESTON SMITH BROOKS and ANDREW PICKENS BUTLER, and famed South Carolina diarist MARY CHESNUT.

Seabrook's modern day cousins include: PATRICK J. BUCHANAN (conservative author), REBECCA GAYHEART (Kentucky-born actress), SHELBY LEE ADAMS (Letcher County, Kentucky, portrait photographer), BERTRAM THOMAS COMBS (Kentucky's fiftieth governor), EDITH BOLLING (wife of President Woodrow Wilson), and actors ROBERT DUVALL, REESE WITHERSPOON, LEE MARVIN, and TOM CRUISE.

Born with music in his blood, Seabrook is an award-winning, multi-genre, BMI-Nashville songwriter and lyricist who has composed some 3,000 songs (250 albums), and whose original music has been heard on TV and radio worldwide. A musician, producer, multi-instrumentalist, and renown performer—whose keyboard work has been variously compared to pianists from HARGUS ROBBINS and VINCE GUARALDI to ELTON JOHN and LEONARD BERNSTEIN—Seabrook has opened for groups such as the EARL SCRUGGS REVIEW, TED NUGENT, and BOB SEGER, and has performed privately for such public figures as President RONALD REAGAN, BURT REYNOLDS, and Senator EDWARD W. BROOKE.

Seabrook's cousins in the music business include: JOHNNY CASH, ELVIS PRESLEY, BILLY RAY and MILEY CYRUS, PATTY LOVELESS, TIM MCGRAW, LEE ANN WOMACK, DOLLY PARTON, PAT BOONE, NAOMI, WYNONNA, and ASHLEY JUDD, RICKY SKAGGS, the SUNSHINE SISTERS, MARTHA CARSON, and CHET ATKINS.

Seabrook lives with his wife and family in historic Middle Tennessee, the heart of Forrest country and the Confederacy, where his conservative Southern ancestors fought valiantly against liberal Lincoln and the progressive North in defense of Jeffersonianism, constitutional government, and personal liberty.

LOCHLAINNSEABROOK.COM

# MEET THE COVER ARTIST

**C**HRISTOPHER ROMMEL is an award-winning Master Caricaturist and freelance illustrator who has been drawing ever since he was old enough to hold a pencil. He is the founder and owner of Exaggerated Entertainment, through which he serves as a party caricaturist for all types of events, including holiday parties, company picnics, birthdays, anniversaries, bar/bat mitzvahs, confirmations, wedding receptions, reunions, banquets, proms, student lock-ins, graduations, open houses, grand openings, trade shows, conventions, conferences, concerts, fund raisers, and boat cruises.

A member of the International Society of Caricature Artists, Rommel won the organization's prestigious "Golden Nosey" award (the Oscar of the caricature industry) for Caricaturist of the Year in 2006. The recipient of numerous other awards for such likenesses as Donald Trump and Christopher Reeve, he is also a nationally published illustrator whose work has appeared in a variety of periodicals and publications, such as *Playboy*, *FHM*, *Flex*, *Exaggerated Features*, and Sea Raven Press.

(Illustration © Chris Rommel)

Rommel launched his career as a professional caricature artist in 1998 when he applied for a summer job at Valleyfair Amusement Park in Shakopee, Minnesota. While employed there he came under the tutelage of renowned *MAD Magazine* artist Tom Richmond. His enrollment at the Academy of Art University in San Francisco, California, as well as two Wisconsin state universities, educated him in a variety of art concentrations. He earned a Bachelor of Fine Arts degree from the University of Wisconsin-Eau Claire in 1999.

Since then, Rommel has drawn some 50,000 live caricatures of people at amusement parks, state fairs, shopping malls, corporate events and private parties. Among his better known clients are Harley-Davidson, Applebee's, Bank of America, Pillsbury, Mars Chocolate, Wells Fargo, First Bank and Trust, Hormel Foods, Petco, Absolut Vodka, Boston Scientific, Walmart and The Home Depot.

Rommel currently resides in Eau Claire, Wisconsin, where he continues to develop both his craft and his well deserved reputation as one of America's premier artists.

**CHRISROMMEL.COM**

If you enjoyed Mr. Seabrook's *The Quotable Nathan Bedford Forrest* you will be interested in his excellent companion works:

*A REBEL BORN: A DEFENSE OF NATHAN BEDFORD FORREST*
*NATHAN BEDFORD FORREST: SOUTHERN HERO, AMERICAN PATRIOT*
*GIVE 'EM HELL BOYS! THE COMPLETE MILIARY CORRESPONDENCE OF NATHAN BEDFORD FORREST*

Available from Sea Raven Press and wherever fine books are sold.

www.ingramcontent.com/pod-product-compliance
Lightning Source LLC
LaVergne TN
LVHW041545070426
835507LV00011B/943